6-

Hospitality
of
the
Heart

Marilyn Brown Oden

PEAK PUBLISHING COMPANY

Montrose, CO

First Edition
Printed in the United States of America

ISBN 1-890437-82-4

Library of Congress No. 2002110337

Cover and text design by Laurie Goralka Design
Cover illustration by Lisa Zador

Peak Publishing Company
P.O. Box 1647
Montrose, CO 81402
www.westernreflectionspub.com

OTHER RECENT BOOKS
BY MARILYN BROWN ODEN

FICTION

Crested Butte: A Novel

NONFICTION

*Abun**dance:***
Joyful Living in Christ

Manger and Mystery:
An Advent Adventure

Through the East Window:
Prayers and Promises for Living with Loss

Wilderness Wanderings:
A Lenten Pilgrimage

For

the good fathers and brothers

at St. Joseph Abbey

St. Benedict, Louisiana

GRATITUDES

This book is based on my "Hospitality of the Heart" presentations for the Fenn Lectureship at Central United Methodist Church in Albuquerque, New Mexico. I am grateful for the opportunity to delve into Christian hospitality, a topic that I had been interested in considering for a long while.

I am grateful for Charles Crutchfield, the outstanding pastor of that church and a leader in United Methodism; for Karen Crutchfield, a talented musician and his partner in ministry; and for the Central congregation and its missional ministry, especially with the homeless.

I am grateful to First United Methodist Church in Dallas, Texas, my home church, where I was privileged to share part of this work for the Women's Retreat.

I am grateful to Highland Park United Methodist Church in Dallas, where I led a Lenten retreat for the Fellowship Sunday School class, and we shared together hospitality of the heart. I especially appreciate Ugonna Onuoha, Betsy Kennard, and Don and Fran Jackson for their help and support.

Four friends were very helpful to me in this writing: The Rev. Katherine Lyle, through discussions; the Rev. Valerie Mireb, through a letter about remembering and forgiving; Johnny Mireb, a Christian born in Palestine, whose capacity for forgiveness stretched my own; and Bishop Rueben P. Job, whose life demonstrates hospitality of the heart. I also want to mention Phil Fenn, a friend of many decades; the Fenn Lectureship honors his father and, therefore, participating in it held a special connection for me.

As always, I am grateful to Bill and our children and grandchildren, who fill my heart with joy.

You're here to be light,

bringing out the God-colors in the world . . .

Shine!

Keep open house;

be generous with your lives.

By opening up to others,

you'll prompt people to open up to God.

— Mt. 5:14, 16 *(The Message)*

CONTENTS

CHAPTER ONE:

Lost!

Deep in the darkness is God.
— Rainer Maria Rilke

I drive along in a rented car, wandering in the dark on a lonely road. The reason is that my plane needed repairs and sat on the tarmac for two hours. Sun and dusk disappeared long ago; and now, as I try to find my way to St. Joseph Abbey, even moon and stars hide behind dense Louisiana clouds. I call Father Dominic to tell him I'll be late. He says he'll be sure the light is left on for me.

Night swallows everything except my lonely headlights. I've been to this Benedictine community before. But that was years ago for a meeting when we lived in Louisiana. And it was in the daytime. Things look so different tonight. Only the smell is familiar, heavy humid air pungent from industrial smokestacks. I think about how long I've yearned for this next step in my faith journey. How I've talked about it and wished for it! (Talking and wishing are so much easier than doing.) Yet, now as I drive toward the abbey, the venture seems surreal rather than real. Especially since I'm wandering around, wrapped in darkness. Lost.

Yes, *lost!* Finally I admit it to myself. I will *really* be late.

I glance at the map, but it doesn't make sense. Somewhere along the way I've taken a wrong fork. I turn around and retrace the road. Finally, I get back on the map once more.

I drive slowly. The isolated road narrows, turns sharply onto the river road, and narrows again. I should be at the abbey by now. It *can't* take this long! Patience is not my strong suit, and impatience wins. I turn too soon. Reach a dead-end. Circle around the gravel road.

And then, at this dead-end as well as my wits' end, I glimpse movement beside the pitch-black circle drive. My headlights flash on two nuns. (Oops! Sisters, not brothers!)

They wave at me in the darkness. "May we help you?" calls one. Her voice holds not even a hint of irritation — though I probably frightened the entire convent.

"I'm sorry. I'm looking for St. Joseph Abbey."

"Go back to the turn," says the second nun kindly. "Proceed a bit further and then you'll see the sign."

I trust and obey. And find the sign . . . the abbey . . . and the light!

Although my very late arrival disturbs the silence of the good monks, that special Benedictine hospitality does not falter. The rule regarding silence is less important than the rule regarding hospitality. Father Dominic warmly welcomes me. He shows me to my room and makes sure all my needs are met, setting up my surroundings in a hospitable way.

"What time do you gather for morning prayers?" I ask.

"Early — 6:15." Considerately, he adds, "You may be too tired to attend."

"Thank you, Father Dominic, but I hunger for the rhythm of worship."

He smiles. "You are welcome to attend."

Father Dominic had just taught me by example the first of many lessons I would learn from this Benedictine community about hospitality of the heart: Hospitality begins with welcoming another as we would welcome the Christ.

LESSON 1: Hospitality begins with welcoming another as we would welcome the Christ.

As he left, gratitude swelled within me to be finally in this holy place, where I'd yearned to come for so long. I looked around the room and noticed the little things provided for my comfort and convenience: a lamp beside the bed, books related to the Rule of St. Benedict on the night stand, and a desk with the daily schedule on it. The next morning after I returned from prayers and heard a ringing sound, I realized that even the alarm clock had been set so I wouldn't miss breakfast.

What a joy, and what a humbling experience it is, to receive the gift of being welcomed as the Christ would be welcomed! It expands our vision of what God created us to become.

Sometimes along life's way we get lost. We get lost in our timidity and our arrogance. In our ignorance and our superiority. We get lost in others' criticism of us and our judgment of others. In our secrets and our self-righteousness. We get lost in our dreams and our despair.

We wander in the dark. The heart-light beckons us onward — not just to talk about a soul goal, not just to wish for it, but to venture toward it. We try to do something we know is right, something we feel called to do. Then things happen that we can't control. Obstacles thwart our way. The journey seems surreal rather than real. The Light seems to disappear. We wander along in our winding way, enveloped in darkness except for the dim flicker deep within our own heart. Things that seem clear in the light look so different in the dark night of the soul. We feel isolated, unsure of our direction. We take wrong turns. The "map" we'd trusted no longer makes sense. But we long to proceed, and we try to make our way back from the deceiving forks we've chosen along the way.

Things seem unfamiliar. We aren't sure about the path. We move ever so slowly. It takes too long. We grow impatient. We turn off too soon. We reach dead-ends.

And we find we need others.

In *The Message*, Eugene Peterson's contemporary version of the Bible, Psalm 22 says:

> *When I left the womb you cradled me;*
> *Since the moment of birth you've been my God.*
> *Then you moved far away*
> *And trouble moved in next-door.*
> *I need a neighbor.*

We need a neighbor. We need each other. We need those who call out to us. Who know we are lost but don't judge us.

Who kindly show us the way and help us set our feet once more in the right direction. We need those who welcome us without mentioning our untimeliness and our disturbance and our disruption of their routine.

We need those who welcome us.

Jesus refers to hospitality in those missional verses from Matthew, cited again and again in congregations: *I was a stranger and you welcomed me . . . When was it that we saw you a stranger and welcomed you?* And we know the answer by heart: *Truly I tell you, just as you did it to one of the least of these . . . you did it to me* (Mt. 25:35, 38, 40). Like so many of us, I attended a prayer service on the evening of that tragic Tuesday — September 11, 2001. The pastor cited those verses and told about a member of his church who was in New York that morning. At the World Trade Center. On the forty-fourth floor. At the time of the attack. Somehow, he got out. A Christian who lived in the city saw him on the street, looked at his scratched face and hands, his sooty and torn clothes, and took this stranger to his own apartment. He gave him something to eat and drink, a place to clean up, some clothes to wear, offered him the phone to call his wife, and let the stranger linger in the apartment. For more than 2000 years Christians have been serving Christ by serving the stranger, giving and receiving hospitality.

During the early centuries of Christianity, a few believers went into the desert to live in solitude. Their withdrawal from the world was not intended, however, to escape from human struggle. They confronted their own inner human frailties and tensions and struggled to overcome their illusions and to purify their hearts. They grew in wisdom — and also reputation. And thus began "the distracting burden of hospitality,"[1] for other Christians (those who felt lost, for example) came to them seeking answers to deep questions. The desert fathers Macarius, Moses, and Poemen, as well as the theologian Evagrius, were great early teachers of the fourth century. Their sayings leave us with awareness that true solitude is about refusing to imprison others in our own projections, not judging them but practicing flexibility in our interpretations of their spiritual lives.[2] It is ironic — or perhaps a natural consequence — that those who had withdrawn from society became sought-after teachers who offered hospitality in the desert, teaching about it and modeling it, welcoming others as the Christ. The stories of the desert fathers (*abbas*) and also a few mothers (*ammas*) still speak to us today:

> During Lent, a brother came to see Abba Poemen, "The Shepherd," and shared his concerns. After finding peace of mind from the old man's wisdom, the brother said, "I almost didn't come to see you today."
>
> "Why?"
>
> "Since it is Lent, I was afraid that the door would not be opened."
>
> Abba Poemen said, "We were not taught to shut wooden doors. The door we need to keep shut is the mouth."[3]

We need people who close their mouths on words of criticism. Who put the rule and spirit of love above lesser rules. Who demonstrate patience with us and seek our well-being. We need those who welcome us as they would welcome the Christ, practicing hospitality of the heart that does not fail them — or us.

And we need God. We may not notice the need for God so much when we know where we are and how to get where we're headed. But we notice it when we feel lost. Abba Macarius, "Blessed One," was asked how to pray. Favoring brevity, he responded, "Say, 'Lord, as you will, and as you know, have mercy.' And if the conflict grows fiercer, say, 'Lord, help!'"[4] We all know that brief and fervent prayer!

Psalm 30 fits us:

> *When things were going great*
> *I crowed, "I've got it made*
> *I'm God's favorite.*
> *He made me king of the mountain."*
> *Then you looked the other way*
> *and I fell to pieces.*

God does not look the other way; we do. God does not move far away from us; we move away from God. And we get ourselves in trouble. And we feel lost. And we yearn to be "found," to be shown the way. *Lord, help!*

A friend told me about an odd experience. Her book club was scheduled to have its November meeting at a woman's house, but when the time came the host found she had to be away. She set up everything before she left. Coffee and tea, mini-muffins and fruit — all beautifully laid out around a Thanksgiving centerpiece.

When people arrived and rang the doorbell, no one answered the door. All the guests just stood around outside, wondering what to do. Someone with a cell phone decided to call the host's number.

The husband answered the phone and apologized. He was supposed to let them in, but he'd been working in the back of the house and hadn't heard the doorbell. After he opened the door and showed them to the goodie table, he returned to his work.

The guests looked askance at each other. Not knowing what to do. Not feeling comfortable. Not sure they should be there. Obviously, the host had gone to a lot of trouble. But they felt strange inside her home in her absence. They didn't really feel *welcome*. Hospitality calls for the presence of a host.

The God of our faith is not an absent host. God did not set the table and leave us. William Ashworth, who has written many books on natural history and the environment, says in *The Left Hand of Eden*, "The finger of God's hand still strokes the universe, disguised as geology."[5] God did not create a once-and-for-all stagnant universe. God's creation is dynamic and continual.

The God of our faith is not an absent host.

Hospitality of the heart begins with God and God's ongoing invitation to the banquet that is always in process — whether or not we remember and respond. Our Creator is the Ultimate Host. We are God's guests. God is always present, always welcoming us, always delighting in us when we show up at the table — just as we delight in our children's presence. We can almost hear God say, "I welcome you, my child. Come close, and feast in faith."

My days at St. Joseph Abbey taught me more about hospitality of the heart than I had learned during all the rest of my life put together. It began so simply: To welcome another as we would welcome the Christ. Then it forked simultaneously in two directions: *to be welcomed* as the Christ and also *to welcome others* as the Christ. As Christian individuals and congregations, we are God's guests and we also serve as God's hosts.

It is interesting to view the movie *Chocolat* from the perspective of hospitality. *Chocolat* is set in a traditional French village ruled by the mayor. At one point boat people come to live on the river near the village. Their values and mores are different from those of the townspeople. Fear of strangers — xenophobia — goes into full swing! The mayor doesn't want the "river rats" in or near his village and calls a town meeting to deal with getting rid of them. Doing so is difficult because they're breaking no laws. The mayor makes a speech suggesting that, even though there are no legal means to handle the problem, there is still one thing the community can do: "We can help them to understand that they are not welcome."

We don't want to admit it but we too, as individuals as well as congregations, know how to help people understand that they are not welcome. Perhaps our "river rats" are those different from us. Or those who don't pass our check sheet of social or economic standards. Or those who challenge our ideas or lifestyles or traditions. Or those who smell. Or the homeless. Whoever our "river rats" are, we help them understand in both overt and subtle ways that they are not welcome. Perhaps, we simply don't invite them.

Let's return to Psalm 22, which goes on to say:

> *Down and outers sit at God's table*
> *And eat their fill.*

All of us are down-and-outers at times. We remember that Jesus himself died *outside* the gate. But how can momentary or permanent down-and-outers, especially folk outside the church, even know about God's table if no one invites them to it and shares with them the good news? How, when they feel empty, can they be filled if individual members and congregations as a whole hold back the bounty? To *say* that the lost, the "down-and-outers," the "River Rats," are welcome at our church table is not the same as *welcoming* them. It is interesting

All of us are down-and-outers at times.

to me that one of the Greek words for stranger is *paroikos*, which can also stand for exile, pilgrim, and sojourner ("River Rat?"). The word for parish is quite similar: *paroikia*, which also conveys a community of pilgrims or sojourners. *All* are welcome!

When we choose to participate in God's banquet, we draw closer to God, receiving and returning God's love. The joy of being invited to God's table shows us the significance of inviting others to our table. We respond to God's gracious love by reflecting it in our own hospitality — welcoming another as we would welcome the Christ.

CHAPTER TWO:

You *Can't* Do Anything Wrong Here

Simply by its presence genuine goodness challenges the best in us.

— David Steindl-Rast

*J*ust before Father Dominic leaves my door on my arrival night at St. Joseph Abbey, he asks, "Can I be of help to you in some way?"

I search his face, not knowing what to say. I'm suddenly aware of my ignorance about monastery life. I'm the only non-resident, the only non-Catholic, the only woman here. I'm afraid I might do something disrespectful or disturbing to the Order. "Is there anything I need to know? I don't want to do anything wrong."

His kind, dark eyes meet mine. "Marilyn, you *can't* do anything wrong here."

❦

LESSON 2: Hospitality offers the gift of a space and place of grace.

This was the second lesson I learned about hospitality of the heart from the Benedictines: Hospitality offers the gift of a space and place of grace.

I hadn't even unpacked yet, and I knew I had already done so many things "wrong." Disrupted and perhaps frightened the sisters up the way. Disturbed the silence of the good brothers and fathers of St. Joseph. And kept Father Dominic waiting up late. All overlooked! *You **can't** do anything wrong here.*

There were no qualifiers. No disclaimers. No small print. He didn't expect me to adopt his beliefs. He didn't even expect me to attend early morning prayers. His grace-filled presence offered compassion and love and acceptance of me just as I am. *Whew!* What a soul-touching experience it is to receive this kind of grace from another!

How often we do things "wrong." Big unalterable things. Small ongoing things. Doing what we shouldn't. Not doing what we should. Like Paul, we long for it to be different. Psalm 40 speaks for us:

> *I'm a mess. I'm nothing and have nothing:*
> *Make something of me.*
> *You can do it; you've got what it takes —*
> *But God, don't put it off.*

Please, God! Don't put it off!

All of us feel like "a mess" at one time or another. During these times especially, we need hospitality of the heart. We need others who lift up our strengths, and we become stronger. Others who love us, and we become more loving. Others who trust us, and we become more trustworthy. Grace from another swings open that little crack in the door to our interior space, where we ourselves can develop the gracious spaciousness needed to offer a grace-filled presence to others.

Likewise, others who do things "wrong" need us. The desert fathers and mothers understood this:

> A brother told the old man, "If I see a monk that I've been told is guilty of a sin, I cannot persuade my soul to bring him into my cell. But if I see a good monk, I gladly bring him in."
>
> The old man said, "If you do good to a good brother, it is little to him. To the other, give twofold, for it is he who is sick."[1]

When others are "a mess," we have an opportunity to be a channel of God's grace. To lift up their strengths even in their weak moments. To love them even in their exasperating moments. To show trust in them even in their mendacious moments. This is no small task; it cuts against what is "due," what is "deserved."

We can learn to avert our eyes.

We can't offer others a space and place of grace if we are focused on what they do "wrong." Pilgrims seeking to grow in faith often asked the desert father Abba John, "What should I do?" Among his suggestions was "control of your eyes."[2] We can learn to avert our eyes. We can focus on something to appreciate instead of something to criticize. I think of a beautiful town where native flowers of yellows and purples and reds brighten the earth and lacey pines give shade. Each morning the sun rises over the mountains and bathes the high desert in gold, and each evening it paints a new masterpiece of pastels across the sky before dipping beneath the horizon. Yet, even there, some residents focus on what is "wrong," spending their days with their heads down like panting Dobermans on a self-imposed chain, sniffing out the area for something to criticize. It might be complaining about a contractor who starts work at the "wrong" time (too early), or a gate painted the "wrong" color (sky tone instead of earth tone), or a car parked in the "wrong" place (in the street). These folk live amidst beauty — and miss it. If we are among those who tend to see what is "wrong" with strangers, neighbors, friends, family, and the world in general, we can learn to change our focus. Focus is a matter of choice.

Not only can we learn to avert our eyes, we can also learn to silence our tongues. When Abba Matoes was asked for wisdom regarding faith, his advice included: "Be aware of your faults; do not judge others" and "put freedom of speech far from you."[3]

We can learn to silence our tongues.

When we choose to focus on and complain about what others do "wrong," we join the long line of people that novelist James Lee Burke (*Bitterroot*) describes as "professional naysayers" who "loved conflict and acrimony so they would not have to contemplate the paucity of significance in their own lives."

Just because we know something, we don't have to tell it. I'm talking not only about confidentialities, but also those little snippets of information gleaned about others over the years. I recall a dinner discussion with several people at a board meeting. We all happened to have connections with a respected and caring gentleman who has a highly prominent public position. Around the table we were sharing our admiration of him. Then the person across from me leaned forward and said to the group, "He's one of my best friends." But the speaker didn't stop there. (How often we precede our little verbal bombs with an expression of friendship!) "We were in school together years ago." He didn't stop there either. "I wonder if his brother is still in prison."

Put freedom of speech far from you. One of the tenets of hospitality of the heart is enacting freedom *from* speech! We are not simply pass-throughs for information about people. It's kinder to keep some things to ourselves. In the movie *Chocolat*, a chocolatier moves into the conventional village, and much to the mayor's dismay her presence begins to alter the old ways and mores. She helps bring about many positive changes in the villagers' lives, increasing his chagrin. Viewing her as a threat to traditional standards, he tries to ruin her business so she will have to leave. He even writes the priest's sermons and includes accusations to turn the villagers against her. My favorite line in the movie comes toward the end. In a fit of rage, having fasted throughout Lent, the mayor breaks into her candy shop the night before

Easter and attacks her beautiful chocolate works of art. When a bit of chocolate lands on his lip, temptation bests him and he breaks his long Lenten fast, gorging on candy. She finds him the next morning passed out in her shop. He has wronged her in many ways, and now she has the goods on him! Looking down at him lying amidst the chocolate ruins, she says, "I won't tell anyone."

Silence about others. A wordless form of grace.

Learning to control our eyes and our tongues is important, but learning to control our thoughts is fundamental. We may not be able to choose our spontaneous thoughts, but we can choose where our minds linger. Abba Poemen said, "A man may seem to be silent, but if his heart is condemning others, he is babbling ceaselessly."[4] Our constant babbling about others' faults (even silently in our hearts) blocks us from seeing our own. It is also a barrier to our awareness of the beauty and goodness around us. Condemning others' "wrongs" fosters a din of hostility rather than a haven of hospitality.

We can learn to control our thoughts.

Sometimes we say, "I had second thoughts about that." Our second thought is significant, especially when the initial one is unkind. A thought pops into our mind; this first thought does not matter so much as the one that follows. It is the second thought that consents or does not consent to the first (and our consent is a choice). The image that comes to me is literally a train of thoughts: When we have an unkind or harmful thought and consent to it, a whole train of critical or angry or demonic thoughts follow along a potentially destructive track. However, when we choose not to consent, our whole train of thought changes and follows a different track.

I'll offer a trivial example: I find that someone I consider pompous is seated next to me at a banquet, and my first thought is *Ugh!* If my second thought consents, I invite a whole train of *ughy* thoughts to travel down a critical track. If, however, my second thought refuses to consent to the *Ugh!*, a new train of thought starts down a different track, one more constructive, one that helps me grow. My refusal to consent gives me an opportunity to become more aware of my own pettiness and immaturity, and to consider what the *Ugh!* reaction points to within myself. (Our negative thoughts always reveal something about *us*.) This new train of thought may even lead to the discovery of characteristics to appreciate in my dinner partner.

Our thoughts are influenced by what we expose our minds to — by where we go and what we do, the things we see and hear, read and watch. Our thoughts are the source of our interpretations of others' words and actions, and these interpretations influence our feelings and attitudes — which in turn influence our interpretations — full circle. Our thoughts both shape and are shaped by our worldview. Paul shows his understanding of the importance of our thoughts: *Finally, beloved, whatever is true, whatever is honorable, whatever is just, whatever is pure, whatever is pleasing, whatever is commendable, if there is any excellence and if there is anything worthy of praise, think on these things* (Phil. 4:8).

You can't do anything wrong here was not the kind of hospitality offered in the Middle East culture of Jesus' day. Xenophobia (*xeno*: stranger; *phobia*: fear) was common. The community viewed strangers as a potential threat to its customs, standards, and safety. They had no influence or protection, and without a host they might simply be ignored or, at worst, never heard from again. Sometimes a letter of recommendation helped. Paul wrote a letter for Phoebe: *I commend to you our sister Phoebe, a deacon of the church in Cenchreae, so that you may welcome her . . . for she has been a benefactor of many and of myself as well* (Rom. 16:1-2). But there were no guarantees. Jesus understood that travel was risky and told his disciples, *If anyone will not welcome you or listen to your words, shake the dust off your feet when you leave that home or town* (Mt. 10:14).

The rigid rules and customs of hospitality in Jesus' culture were like a choreographed dance between host and guest. Missteps on the part of either could jeopardize the whole. For example, the host (a male head of the family) must grant guests their due honor, and guests must not assume an honored place. We recall Jesus' words, *When you are invited by someone to a wedding banquet, do not sit down at the place of honor, in case someone more distinguished than you has been invited by your host* (Lk. 14:8). The host must protect guests and regard an offense against them as an offense against himself, and guests must honor the host and not embarrass him by finding another host. Jesus instructed the disciples: *Whatever town or village you enter, find out who in it is worthy, and stay there until you leave* (Mt. 10:11). The host must not neglect guests' needs and wishes, and guests must not usurp the host's role or give orders to his family. When Jesus was in someone's home, he healed only when asked to do so. The host must offer his best in order not to denigrate guests, and guests must not take something unoffered or refuse something offered — especially food. Furthermore, both host and guests must avoid insults, hostility, and rivalry.

During this dance, guests began to tell stories about where they were from, the places they'd been, and their adventures during the journey. These stories unveiled a broadened world for the host, now dependent on the guest for making the unknown known. For the moment, the guest became the host and the host became the guest, bringing more balance to the relationship.

As a guest's misstep in the dance risked loss of protection, a host's misstep risked loss of reputation. Paul often spoke well of his hosts: *When we arrived at Jerusalem, the brothers welcomed us warmly* (Acts 21:17). He mentioned Publius, *who received us and entertained us hospitably for three days* (Acts 28:7). And Gaius, *whose hospitality I and the whole church here enjoy* (Rom.16:23 NIV). But poor Diotrephes! In the Book of John, his reputation as a poor host is laid before all of Christendom: *I wrote to the church, but Diotrephes, who loves to be first, will have nothing to do with us. So if I come, I will call attention to what he is doing, gossiping maliciously about us. Not satisfied with that, he refuses to welcome the brothers. He also stops those who want to do so and puts them out of the church* (3 Jn. 1:9-10). Apparently, Diotrephes did not silence his tongue or avert his eyes!

The host took the first step in the dance by offering food and inviting guests to wash their feet. They had walked for miles in sandals along the dusty roads of Palestine, and this was a refreshing gesture of hospitality. It was also part of Jesus' religious heritage, learned from the Torah. Abraham said to his three visitors, *Let a little water be brought, and wash your feet, and rest yourselves under the tree* (Gen. 18:4). Lot told the two angels who arrived in Sodom, *You can wash your feet and spend the night and then go on your way early in the morning* (Gen.19:2). Simon omitted this gesture when Jesus went to his home. Perhaps Jesus wouldn't have mentioned it if Simon had not also rebuked the kind woman, after which Jesus told him: *I entered your house; you gave me no water for my feet, but she has bathed my feet with her tears and dried them with her hair. You gave me no kiss, but from the time I came in she has not stopped kissing my feet. You did not anoint my head with oil, but she has anointed my feet with ointment* (Lk. 7:44-46).

When Jesus washed the disciples' feet during the Last Supper, he transformed this ancient foot-washing tradition into a sign of servanthood for Christians. Some three hundred years after Jesus walked the Palestinian hillsides, monks from Jerusalem visited Abba Apollo in Egypt and described his hospitality. After bowing, kissing them, and praying, he "washed our feet with his own hands. He urged us to rest ourselves and eat, for it was his custom to do this to all the brothers who came to visit him."[5] Many congregations today continue this tradition by including foot-washing in special Lenten services.

The new believers were excited about Jesus' teachings and wanted to share the good news. Hospitality was especially important as they traveled to different places trying to spread their faith. Paul says, *Practice hospitality* (Rom. 12:13 NIV).

By the time we get to 1 Peter, written about two to three generations later, we see that a phrase has been added: *Offer hospitality to one another **without grumbling*** (1 Pet. 4:9 NIV).

In the early church, hospitality included charity. Many hospitals, orphanages, and leprosariums grew out of Christian hospitality. Possessions were regarded as gifts to be shared with others, and hospitality was a high priority. A desert father visited a sheepherder and his wife, Eucharistus and Mary. Eucharistus told him, "Here are these sheep; we received them from our parents, and if, by God's help we make a little profit, we divide it into three parts: one for the poor, the second for hospitality, and the third for our personal needs."[6] No paltry tithe for Eucharistus and Mary!

Jesus' words and actions showed that he knew his culture's choreographed dance of hospitality. Yet, he dared to introduce new and shocking steps — he included Gentiles (non-Jews) and women and placed grace before rules. Abba Poemen's wisdom speaks to us when we are tempted by a pre-Jesus focus on others' keeping the rules rather than on our offering grace:

Jesus moved us from rule-guardians to love-bearers.

A brother visited him, seeking his advice: "Some brothers live with me," he told the old man. "Do you want me to be in charge of them?"

Abba Poemen said, "No. Be their example, not their legislator."[7]

Jesus moved us from rule-guardians to love-bearers. His life taught us a new dance, one to the music of inclusivity and grace. Over the centuries hospitality has become a spiritual discipline for Christians and an important characteristic of a community of faith.

Yet, xenophobia lingers in our world today, affecting hospitality. Think about our emphasis on suspicion and its effect on our children. Part of our xenophobia is now due to that tragic Tuesday of 2001. But long before, we were sending our school children through metal detectors and training them regarding what to do if they hear gunshots — a process resulting from our own homegrown, gun-toting children.

We tend to forget that our national news reaches international stations. I have watched U.S. news in various parts of the world, oftentimes with my hosts. They are courteous and try to hide their horror, but they cannot fathom how children can have access to guns, how they can manage to take them to school without their parents' knowledge, how they can use them to kill other children. In some of these countries, not even police or prison guards carry guns. It is scary for ordinary people — who recognize us as the most powerful nation in the world — to view our news and see our violence. The distorted international view of our country and its citizens is understandable because our own media spews our violence across the airwaves way out of proportion to our amazing benevolence.

It is likely that "Stranger Danger" shapes more children today than "Jesus Loves Me." How do we find a balance? In *The Silent Roots*, K. M. George reminds us that in traditional non-industrialized societies, children are joyful when visitors arrive from another place, for they open up an exciting new world. Children listen to the stories they tell. "A sense of mystery surrounds" them, not suspicion.[8] I found this to be true in a United Methodist school in a remote area of Zimbabwe. The little African children stared at me, ever so curious. I realized that I might be the only Anglo person they had ever seen. So I smiled at them and extended an open palm. They descended on me! Touching me. Patting me. Feeling my hair. Not at all fearful, suspicious, xenophobic. Their beautiful smiles were radiant. Their eyes hid nothing. Those children are terribly "poor," but they are rich in the precious gift of enjoying the mystery of a stranger. How different it is in our country today! The church may be the only place where our children can be with strangers they are not taught to distrust. If that is the case, this is a crucial and timely congregational ministry.

A frequent "older generation" topic of conversation is how the world is changing — and how much worse it is "now" than it was "then." A story from the desert fathers demonstrates that nearly two thousand years ago, people also shook their heads at the shameful worsening of the world:

> One seeking wisdom asked an old man, "How is it that some struggle away at their religious life, but do not receive grace like the old fathers?"
> The old man said, "Because then charity ruled, and each one drew his neighbour upward. Now charity

is growing cold, and each of us draws his neighbour
downward, and so we do not deserve grace."[9]

No, we don't deserve grace. Not then. Not now. God's
grace has always been a gift. It still is. God's grace does not
change — and neither, apparently, does the human view that
our "then" world was better than our "now" world. Wringing
our hands and creasing our brow, we bemoan that things and
people are getting worse — that charity is growing cold and
neighbors are drawn downward. This dismal view is one of the
few constants in two millennia. What's new is the speed and
spread of reporting human misdeeds.

Mass media helps tip the scales toward mistrust of our fellow human beings, for it suffers from a cast-suspicion syndrome,
repetitive soundbyte reductionism, and hyperbolical headlines
like "America is on edge this morning!" (And if we didn't wake
up "on edge," we will be by the time the report concludes.) The
news is skewed toward the negative: "If it bleeds, it leads."
Murders, rapes, and robberies. And these stories begin to shape
our perspective of the world (and, as stated earlier, the international community's perception of us).

Let's draw back for a moment from this daily bread of sen-
sationalism and look at the reality of our own personal experiences. Without discounting the horrible pain and suffering of
victims of crime — whether ourselves, our friends, or strangers
— let's consider for the moment the frequency of crime experi-
enced in our own personal lives. How many thousands (hundreds of thousands) of people have you encountered,
cumulatively, in your life? Ever been to a sports arena with
50,000 others? Or packed yourself body-to-body on Canal

Street in New Orleans for Mardi Gras? Or ridden a subway during rush hour? How many times? And how many of those strangers committed a criminal act against you? The overwhelming odds are *none* of them. During your entire life, considering all the people whose hands you've shaken and all the strangers you've passed beside, how many tried to murder, rape, or rob you? The masses fall somewhere between villains and heroes, which makes the overall percentage of villains so small that we can wake up proud to be part of the human race!

What is your personal experience? I'll share mine. During my entire life, with the hundreds of thousands of strangers and friends who have been in my midst, my only encounter with a murderer occurred when visiting a prison. Two rapists have touched my life: A friend of mine was a victim on a college campus, and I served on a jury that convicted a man of rape. Two thieves have given me grief: One stole cash from my dorm room in Oxford, England. The other — well, the other is a story that merits telling.

During Advent my arms were full of presents to mail as my husband Bill and I approached a post office inside a grocery store. Suddenly, a man grabbed my purse and all the presents dropped.

None of this passive stuff for us! We chased him. I caused all the commotion I could. Screaming **HELP!** and running after him and shrieking as loud as an Amtrak train. But not as fast. Bill and I could never have caught him.

But a stranger joined us. And another. Then another. The chase was on — five to one! But that thief had speed! He rounded a corner. Where'd he go? Home free, I thought. Suddenly a man dressed in medic greens jumped out of his truck, right in the middle of the road. He darted between two businesses. Grabbed the thief scaling a fence. Pulled him down by his feet and tackled him. One of the other three men called the police on his cell phone. The man in medic greens straddled the villain, now face down on the ground, and took the purse. He handed it to me with a smile and said, "I'm so grateful! All during Advent, I've been praying that I'd get a chance to help somebody!"

That story didn't make the news.

We've already considered how few criminals there are among our overall population masses. My personal experience paints an even brighter picture. When the chase is on, watch out, villains! The heroes have it, four to one!

You may have fared better or worse than I. The point is to be wary of letting the skewed news damage our perception of God's children. The habitual emphasis on fear and gloom (potentially self-fulfilling) turns the newsroom into the doom room. If we are not consciously purposeful about seeing the face of Jesus in others, we could easily become unconsciously pro-grammed to see the face of Judas instead.

Xenophobia, excessive suspicion, and automatic fear are heart blockages. They block the Spirit and our flow of love that enable us to offer a space and place of grace. Wisdom and discernment are necessary, of course, both to sense when to be cautious and when fear is unmerited. The more habitually xenophobic, suspicious, and fearful we become, the more important it is that

Xenophobia, excessive suspicion, and automatic fear are heart blockages.

the church heal our hearts through the Gospel message *Do not be afraid*.

Hospitality of the heart is an inclusive dance of grace for individual Christians and congregations as a whole. We walk through life with different dreams and difficulties, in various stages of happiness and hardship, and with assorted sources of anticipation and anxiety. But whoever we are, and whenever we were born, and whatever our state at the moment, we hold one thing in common: We have a deep yearning for hospitality of the heart.

We long for release from rigid rules and the choreographed dance where missteps are noted. Where mistakes are measured, and scores are settled. Where hostility hovers, and rivalry rattles the soul. Where insults impede, and honor is limited to what is "due."

We long for hospitality that transcends our human foibles and accepts us without conditions. Hospitality that rises above debate and argument and a win-lose mentality and that puts comforting the other above competing with the other.

We long for hospitality in which the only ultimate rule is the rule of love. An empowering, freeing, nonmanipulative rule. A rule that is not a rule at all but a response. A response to the amazing all-encompassing love of God, a love that inspires and energizes us toward becoming our best self. A self that does not simply absorb God's love but reflects it to others. Offering open minds, open hearts, open doors. Offering the healing presence of a space and place of grace where another *can't* do anything wrong.

CHAPTER THREE:

We've Been Talking

*As we open our creative channel
to the Creator,
many gentle but powerful changes
are to be expected.*
— Julia Cameron

An elderly brother is the only one in the beautiful sanctuary when I arrive early for vespers. He sees me and smiles. Though he has difficulty walking on his lame legs, he begins to come toward me, carefully and laboriously making his way down the chancel steps. "Is it OK to tease?" he asks.

I return his smile. "Of course."

"We've been talking," he says, his eyes twinkling. "We are wondering about something." He softens his voice, conspiratorially. "What would your bishop-husband think if you convert to Catholicism?" Delighted with his joke, his laughter fills this sacred place like a joyful hymn to the smiling Holy One.

I laugh with him. Yet, his words cascade ever so lightly over my soul, and I realize that they are not totally without merit. As I walk these hallowed grounds, conducive to ongoing inner transformation, I am aware of experiencing conversion of my life, for a subtle change is occurring deep within me.

This was the third lesson I learned about hospitality of the heart from the Benedictines: Hospitality has the power to bring change to both receiver and giver.

LESSON 3: Hospitality has the power to bring change to both receiver and giver.

As Jesus journeyed through arid Palestine, he showed openness, compassion, and tenderness to Jews and Gentiles (non-Jews) alike. He didn't let his vision fall victim to the perceptions of those around him. He overcame the prejudices and passions of his culture and offered a new path to follow. He brought healing waters for individuals' fragmented, broken lives, restoring connection and integration — integrity — of their body-mind-spirit. He offered the gift of wholeness — holiness of heart. Jesus did not denounce the world; he announced potential transformation of people. Hospitality is one of the channels for our transformation, both through giving hospitality and receiving it.

Hospitality of the heart is holistic, including hospitality to the self. This relates to the process of becoming whole, integrated in body/mind/soul. In *The Man Who Killed the Deer*, a

> **Hospitality of the heart is holistic, including hospitality to the self.**

novel by Frank Waters, the Kiva chiefs speak, "There are three understandings: of the body, of the head, of the heart. What endures must be understood by all."

We offer hospitality to the self by caring for our bodies. We can give ourselves the gifts of exercise and good nutrition. (For me, that means hitting the walking trail instead of the cookie jar when I'm stuck on writing something.) Our bodies are wonderful miraculous creations of God, allowing us to do all that we do, integrating our myriad parts into a functioning whole, healing and restoring us. Paul speaks of the body as a temple of the Holy Spirit within us, which we have from God (1 Cor. 6:19). Our body is a *temple* — whatever size and shape, however young or old. Whether we have the graceful agility of an Olympics skater or totter along with the help of a walker, our bodies deserve to be honored. How we treat them is one of the ways that we show reverence to our Creator.

We offer hospitality to the self by caring for our minds. We can give ourselves the gift of time to read good novels and see good movies. To savor gifts that catch us by surprise in the moment — a beautiful sunset or the way sunbeams rain down, red and golden. To savor sounds — fall leaves crunching underfoot or the magic of poetry read aloud. To savor smells — musty trunks and dusty attics, lilacs and lilies, evening rain and fresh-mowed grass. We can give ourselves the privilege of changing what we think, for we are empowered to make new observations and reinterpret old ones. We can give ourselves opportunities to enjoy mental challenges, to ponder diverse ideas, and to weigh the impact of multidimensional changes around the globe (political, technological, economical, ecological, and all the other "-icals") that affect specific cultures and the human spirit in general. In her introduction to *The Flowering of the Soul*, Lucinda Vardey says, "The many gifts of the mind — predominantly reason, observation, and judgment — can be used to discern the imprint of the Divine and the needs and aspirations of the soul."[1]

We also offer hospitality to the self by caring for our souls, deepening our relationship with God. We can give ourselves the gifts of solitude and reflection. The gift of studying the scriptures and the spiritual classics. The gift of prayer, all kinds of prayers — contemplative prayer and congregational prayer, prayers of words and works, prayers of silence and service, prayers that look and listen for the ways God speaks to us. Our spiritual unfolding isn't instantaneous — like a magician's snapping open a paper flower. Time is necessary to become aware of God's benevolent power in our lives. The unfolding of our spiritual dimension is not a matter of wish or will. Or merely a matter of decision and discipline. Or even a matter of seeking, for the journey brings us back to the center.

Our spiritual dimension unfolds as we desire a deeper relationship with God enough to act on this desire, giving our time and attention to this relationship, growing in it, learning from it, responding to it in gratitude, and embracing it in our daily living. Soul care is an ongoing, lifelong process.

Our integration of body, mind, and soul includes pleasure and delight. We bask in gratitude and respond in joy. We play.

We have fun. We laugh. Gratitude and joy come from within, and we reflect them in our exterior space — like the good monk who, in spite of his lame legs, approaches others with twinkling eyes and soul-deep laughter and the ever-present hope for the possibility of conversion.

Hospitality of the heart helps refocus our self-centeredness. Thomas Kelly, who was a Quaker professor of philosophy, wrote to his wife about a "gentle, loving, but awful Power. And it makes one know the reality of God at work in the world. And it takes away the old self-seeking, self-centered self." He asked her help "not to be proud of learning, not ambitious for self, but emptied of these things, and guided by that amazing Power, which is so gentle." He confessed, "We have been so hardened, so crusted, so worldly-wise. I have been so self-seeking . . ."[2]

And I too will confess: So have I. Perhaps this confession is also yours. Maybe it is everyone's.

I'll share a secret with you: To the degree that we experience centeredness within the self — being in touch with the Holy Spirit within us, which we have from God — we are

> **To the degree that we experience centeredness within the self, we are emptied of self-centeredness.**

emptied of self-centeredness. Again: We are emptied of self-centeredness to the degree that we experience centeredness within the self. Kelly speaks of finding ourselves "continually recreated, and realigned and corrected again and again from warping effects of outer affairs." He says it is a matter of "having a Center of creative power and joy and peace and creation" within us.[3]

This Center, this holy place within, is always accessible to us, no matter where we are or what we are doing. The more we visit it, the more it calls to us and comforts us and challenges us. As we go through life, we unavoidably grow less and less attractive physically. But age blesses us with the opportunity to reach deeper and deeper into our spirituality and grow more and more beautiful of soul.

Oh, yes! Hospitality can change us.

One aspect of the Rule of St. Benedict is "Conversion of Life," a *metanoia*, an ongoing inner transformation. St. Benedict said: "Your way of acting should be different from the world's way; the love of Christ must come before all else. You are not to act in anger or nurse a grudge. Rid your heart of all deceit. Never give a hollow greeting of peace or turn away someone who needs your love."[4] Hospitality of the heart fosters our inner transformation as individual Christians and as congregations.

Hospitality can open our minds and soften our hardness of heart. It can shrink our fears and broaden our tolerance. It can

> **Hospitality can open our minds and soften our hardness of heart.**

encourage us toward relinquishing our need to control situations and other people. It invites us to risk giving up our tidy, deadening narrow-mindedness. It sets before us the opportunity for relationships with those who are different from us, who disagree with us, and even with those we call "foes." It loosens the boundaries of our comfortable categories, challenges our habitual behaviors, and confronts our dearly held traditions that are harmful to others. Above all, hospitality of the heart deepens our awareness of the astounding abundance of God's gifts as the Ultimate Host.

Oh, yes! Hospitality can change us.

One of the ways hospitality brings change is through stories. Hospitality and stories go together. Human beings have been telling stories since the beginning of time and depicting them on ancient walls from the moment someone in the clan created a way to do it. When stories are told, memories are made. And the memories themselves later become stories to tell.

Stories touch our hearts and alter our perceptions, allowing us to acknowledge views of the world different from our own. I recall a story about a teacher who asked for a volunteer to use the word "unaware" in a sentence. A little boy raised his hand, "Our unaware is the last thing we take off at night and the first thing we put on in the morning." The lad may have confused *unaware* with *underwear*, but his comment was profound. How often we don *unawareness* the first thing in the morning and remove it the last thing at night! Stories awaken awareness.

The monks were telling a story about me. Now, I'm telling stories about the monks. Life ripples through our stories, from person to person, from generation to generation. There is great power in exchanging stories. It builds bridges to one another, for when we share our stories we are no longer strangers. We can't be — for we share our souls in our stories.

When we share our stories we are no longer strangers.

In my fantasy of fantasies, the plane highjackers and passengers tell each other their stories on that tragic Tuesday of 2001. And the stories of the passengers melt a tiny hole in the chilled souls of the killers. But it is enough. It is enough. Through that tiny hole trickles the memory of their own stories before the ice age of hate struck them. Memories of being held on their mothers' laps. Memories of learning the verses of love and peace in the Quran. Memories of a life worth living. And in my utopian fantasy of fantasies, they do not commit murder, and the passengers go home to their loved ones, and the twin towers still stand.

That's how my pen would write it. Would that it were so!

Holidays are a great time for stories. Somehow sitting around the table gives us permission to stretch our feats a bit, exaggerate our triumphs just a tad, and color our ordinary actions with a wash of heroism. My husband's mother loved to tell stories. When I was younger, it always bothered me that she didn't stick to the facts. If she were alive today, I would thank her for her stories, her wonderfully embellished stories.

I was walking through a mall and overheard a woman saying to her husband, "It will make a great story. I can hardly wait to tell them. They'll love it!"

I still wonder what that story was!

We all have stories. And some of them we can hardly wait to tell. For example, something happened last summer that made me feel like a child again. It was insignificant, but it brought back childlike joy, and I've wanted to tell someone that story. It appears to be pointless and unrelated to this writing, and maybe it is. But it's a story that wants to be told, so perhaps it reveals a bit of my soul — the part that can still be childlike.

Last summer Bill and I rode the night train from Madrid to Paris because it cost less than the plane. I took the upper berth — I'd rather fall on him than he on me! Up I went, and discovered that I had my own little lamp and shelf, and I could see out the window. The train rumbled and rocked, and sometimes stopped. That was the best part. Curious, I would plop to the end of the little bed, sit cross-legged, and peek out — seeing but unseen, like a small child hidden in the background, observing strangers from my unobserved place. What was the town like, this town that lay quiet late at night, this town with its dim depot lights flickering in the darkness? Who were the people departing? Boarding? What stories could they tell? Not knowing (but hoping to write mysteries one day), I made up my own stories about them. And unbeknownst to them, they were transformed into heroes — and a few into villains. (Even as I write this at three o'clock in the morning, a night train wails on the nearby tracks. It used to be a mournful sound to me. Now, it beckons me toward a journey of mystery.)

Ahh! If only we could become as excited and filled with childlike wonder about *The Story!* The story that can change our lives. If only we as congregations could hardly wait to tell that story!

We could all tell stories about our experiences of hospitality as a host or a guest. Perhaps we remember receiving a special welcome. Or we were offered a moment of grace. Or something happened that brought insight and the beginning of change. It is not so much the smooth surface of an impressive evening that opens the door to hospitality of the heart and change in us. It is more likely the knotholes, the surprises, the unexpected.

When our four children were little and Bill was a pastor in Oklahoma City, the Council of Bishops met there. The word (or warning) went out across Oklahoma: "The bishops are coming! The bishops are coming!" One of them, whom we had never met personally, was highly regarded by us and our group of young clergy friends. So Bill and I mustered our courage and invited him to a dinner party with about thirty friends.

I wanted to have an impressive party for this esteemed bishop and worked hard on the dinner. I remember being somewhat scared and hoping for a bit of dignity in the atmosphere.

About halfway through dinner, one of our children came running downstairs. "Mom!" he yelled. "Shambray is having kittens!"

Our four children spent a good part of the evening shouting over the banister with a blow-by-blow description, "One is halfway out!"

(There went dignity!)

Shambray took most of the evening giving birth to six kittens during that party. And I spent a good part of the evening upstairs with the children, Shambray, and the new kittens.

That night I was not the one who offered hospitality of the heart. My children did. While I was into impressing a bishop, they were into the miracle of life. And seeing that, something began to change in me.

Oh, yes! Hospitality can change us.

When we think of log cabins and farmhouses and homes from a previous century, our nostalgic image includes porches. Often big, wraparound porches. Even King Solomon had a porch. (Check it out: 1 Kings 7:6.) But somewhere along the way (perhaps with the advent of the light bulb, radio, television, and air conditioning), friendly porches were reduced to thresholds too small for rocking chairs and porch swings. We traded in a place to tell stories and wave at the neighbors across the street for a silent place in front of TV, a medium geared to the lowest common marketing mentality. Hospitality provides an opportunity to tell stories, transforming a "threshold" once again into a "wraparound porch."

Every single day provides an opportunity to tell a new story with our words and our actions. We don't have to retell yesterday's story or be stuck in yesterday's pattern or walk through the new day in yesterday's rut. Each sunrise invites us to see the past as an introduction to the real beginning of our story, a story that can be part of the contemporary version of The Story. Hospitality offers us the gift of others' presence. We still walk our individual lives, but we do so

> **Each sunrise invites us to see the past as an introduction to the real beginning of our story.**

telling stories and sharing joy, weeping and laughing together, holding hands and touching souls.

Yes, my dear monk with the wounded legs and the wonderful laugh, even though I will remain a United Methodist, I am being converted — changed — through hospitality of the heart.

CHAPTER FOUR:

Beautiful
Hands

Maybe the place where the gap has to be bridged is within me.

— Henri J. M. Nouwen

While sitting in my room one night at St. Joseph Abbey, I thumb through a book that tells about the monastery. A picture of Father Dominic in his younger years catches my eye. He is directing the choir. I know the sound through CDs — music filled with praise, music of holiness and adoration, music that picks me up and carries me toward the Spirit of God. In the photograph Father Dominic is smiling as he directs, his hands lifted.

Beautiful hands. Artistic hands. Magical hands. Serving God through music.

Arriving early for lauds the next morning, I watch him prepare for me. Father Dominic now serves God in another way. He still sings beautifully, but he directs the oblates[1] instead of the choir, and he offers hospitality of the heart to guests. For example, he always has the appropriate worship sheets at my place. My *place*, where his nod invites me to come and sit with the fathers and brothers right up there by the altar. He has everything ready so that I won't be confused during this holy time, so common for them, so unfamiliar for me — a non-Catholic, a woman, a newcomer who doesn't know what to do. Because of his caring hospitality, I'm able to participate fully in each sacred time of worship.

As I watch, I notice for the first time the arthritis in his joints. His hands testify to the pain he endures silently. Yet, those aching fingers sort through the prayers and psalms, finding the right ones and putting them in the proper order. All during my stay, he takes this extra time and effort for me. Each day. Four times a day. His hands — older than the unaged ones in the photograph — are still busy, still lifted, still praising. But now they reveal his courage and character.

Beautiful hands. Caring hands. Faithful hands. Serving God through hospitality.

This was the fourth lesson I learned about hospitality of the heart while being with the Benedictines: Hospitality is the measure of beautiful hands.

LESSON 4: Hospitality is the measure of beautiful hands.

Gnarled or mottled hands are beautiful when offering hospitality. As are hands calloused by work or crippled by disease. And hands with swollen knuckles or missing fingers, and hands crystal-fragile or quarterback-strong. All hands are beautiful that serve God through hospitality.

Each of us has images of beautiful hands. Three mental snapshots come to mind. A feeble grandparent tottering along on a sidewalk, hand-in-hand with a beloved toddler. A friend clasping his mother's hand at the funeral of her other son. My husband taking his dying father's hand for the last time and hearing the final word he would speak: "Son." Beautiful hands enfold others' hands.

Mother Grimes, a good Christian woman who took me under her wing when I was a new bride, donned an apron to make German chocolate cake from "scratch." Jesus wrapped a towel around his waist to wash the disciples' feet. Robed clergy oftentimes wear a stole, symbolic of that towel and servant-hood. Beautiful hands unfold in care.

We reflect our connection to God by connecting to the world — *in* but not *of* — this complex world. As followers of Christ, we are not only God's guests, but also hosts on God's behalf among God's children. We are invited to offer hospitality as we go about our everyday experiences — while at work, ballgames, waiting in line, even driving in traffic. Paul says: *Through us spreads in every place the fragrance that comes from knowing him.* Wherever we walk, individually as Christians and corporately as congregations, we have an opportunity to spread *the aroma of Christ* (2 Cor. 2:14-15). The Benedictines of St. Joseph do this literally, for one of the many ways they serve others is by baking bread for the homeless. Each time I catch a whiff of warm bread, I think of the monks' hospitality — both within and beyond the abbey.

I recall the memorial service for Bill May, a pastor in our area. He was the kind of person we especially don't want to die — it leaves the earth a lesser place. When we left his small church, my husband pointed to the sign above the door that led outside: SERVANTS ENTRANCE. Oftentimes we don't understand today's world, and we feel confused about how to respond faithfully to complex issues. Yet, one thing is clear: As Christians, we enter the world through the "Servants' Entrance," extending our beautiful hands in hospitality.

> **As Christians, we enter the world through the "Servants' Entrance."**

We also have images of beautiful hands folding in prayer. Psalm 71 asks God to

> *Be a guest room where I can retreat;*
> *you said your door was always open!*

Suppose we turn that around and see prayer as beautiful hands offering hospitality to God, inviting the Host to be our guest, to abide in our inner guest room. We don't ignore our guests! Prayer is a time to focus our concentration on awareness of God's presence. According to Simone Weil, a political activist and spiritual writer, prayer "is the orientation of all the attention of which the soul is capable towards God."[2] If we treat God as well as we treat other guests, we won't spend the whole time of prayer carrying on a monologue, or whining and complaining, or begging and bargaining.

Following a time of prayer, we may want to invite others to join us at the table — people we can learn from in the scriptures as well as people who came later and used their beautiful hands in remarkable ways. After we have read their stories and the saints have excused themselves, we may sense that our Honored Guest doesn't want to spend *all* the time we share simply sitting around. Let's go do something together! Something that acts out hospitality of the heart. Something that we feel led toward by our Guest.

Hospitality of the heart stems from our awareness of God's presence. It is our gift to give when we are centered in the Spirit and praying silently for God to be in our looking and listening. This gift of hospitality is beyond the superficial, for it relates to our *heart*, the very core of our being, our center without facade. It links our deeds to the spirit behind them. An old man of the desert made this point by telling a story about a priest who was reputed to be "generous in almsgiving" but did so with "a mean spirit":

A widow came to ask the priest for a little barley. He said to her, "Go and fetch a measure, and I will weigh you some."

She did so, but when the priest weighed the measure in his hand he said, "It is too big." And he made her ashamed.

After she had gone, I said, "Priest, did you lend barley to that widow, or what?"

"No," he said. "I gave it to her."

But I said, "If you wanted to make her a free gift, why were you so exact about the measure, making her ashamed?"[3]

The priest gave, but not with a generous spirit. He offered hospitality without the heart.

I know a grandfather who used his beautiful hands to build a playhouse for his grandchildren to enjoy when they came to visit. He built a table and chairs scaled down to childsize because, just as he viewed the altar table to be the center of the church, he viewed the dining table to be the center of the home.

His grandchildren loved to play there. One day he was rocking contentedly on the porch, watching them through the playhouse door and windows. They were all sitting down at the table except his oldest granddaughter, who held a notepad and pencil. She was going around from one child to another, talking to each one for a moment and writing something down.

Curious, he ducked into the playhouse. "What are you doing?"

"We're having a special family dinner," said one of the boys. The grandfather was puzzled.

"She's taking our orders at the restaurant," another explained.

These children were practicing what is commonplace in our culture — hospitality without the hands. There's nothing wrong with this. Everyone is busy, and restaurant hospitality is much easier and less time consuming than home hospitality. Without it, we might not get together at all. I recall many special and memorable meals with family and friends at restaurants.

Yet, offering our hands with our hospitality adds a special personal touch. We can set up the exterior space in a way that invites a sharing together of interior space. And isn't that the deep hope — sharing our inner space?

The table is a great equalizer.

Suppose we want to have some friends in for dessert or a cookout or a dinner party. It can be risky! In my novel, *Crested Butte*, a coal miner's widow decides to have the visiting coal baron for dinner. When her friend expresses surprise, she explains, "Heffron looks down on miners . . . I want to put faces on them so he will see them as persons. I want us to sit around the table together as equals." The table is a great equalizer.

Hospitality at home takes time and calls for many decisions: Whom to invite — and leave out. How to invite them. Whether to consider individual needs. How to set up the room and the table. How much attention to give the senses — like the sight of candle flames and centerpiece, the sound of background music, the smell of bread baking and coffee making. Our preparations can result in a whole-hearted WELCOME sign. Unintentionally, however, they can also result in a scattering of small-print NO TRESPASSING signs.

The key is our focus. Are we focused on guests or self? Esther de Waal (*Seeking God*) says: "I know that soon four people will be sitting round the table sharing the meal. If I am actually afraid and defensive (or aggressive, which is much the same), anxious and insecure about the

Hospitality of the heart is never about impressing someone; it is about caring for someone.

impression that I shall be making, I may offer a glass of sherry or a bowl of soup but any real hospitality of the heart will be lacking; I shall have merely fulfilled the social expectation."[4] How easy it is to trip over our anxiety about making a good impression! Hospitality of the heart is never about impressing someone; it is about caring for someone.

Setting up the exterior space is not the end; it is the means for inviting others to cross the bridge over the moat to our interior space. The props are less important than an atmosphere of acceptance that invites authentic dialogue. We want to offer an opportunity to share deeply together during these few hours — hours of our lives never again to be lived. De Waal continues, "I cannot become a good host until I am at home in my own house, so rooted in my centre . . . that I no longer need to impose my terms on others but can instead afford to offer them a welcome that gives them a chance to be completely themselves."[5] We offer the gift of our deep self to another's deep self.

The condition of our inner space affects our exterior space. Our capacity to offer a more gracious — grace-filled —

presence is enlarged as our inner space becomes deeper and more expansive. I picture our inner space to be like a maturing orchard of the fruits of the Spirit: love, joy, and peace; patience, kindness, and goodness; gentleness, faithfulness, and self-control (Gal. 5:22). These sacred fruits grow primarily through the sunlight of God's grace. Our part is to hoe the weeds and attend to our relationship with the Creator.

When the evening is over and our guests go home, they take something with them and leave something behind with us. It's always the same: A *memory*. We hope that it is a memory of being refreshed and of sensing peace and of sharing deeply, a memory that will bring a smile of pleasure, a memory that will be recalled long after one of us has moved far away — or perhaps even died.

Congregational hospitality can also be risky. The altar table, like the dining table, is a great equalizer. Psalm 15 asks:

> *God, who gets invited*
> *To dinner at your place?*
> *How do we get on your guest list?*

Congregational hospitality takes time and planning, attention to the atmosphere, and consideration of the tone set by the leaders. It requires an honest look at the practice of grace, at the focus of the congregation, at openness to change and diversity, and at xenophobia. It also calls for a look at the invitation list. My friend Char told me about a woman whose son was sentenced to prison. Shortly afterward the mother received a letter from her church asking her not to continue participating. We bristle! But before we denounce that church, let's admit that in every city there are people who have loved ones in prison. Are they on our congregational invitation list?

Suppose we do put all kinds of people on this list, including down-and-outers, and our congregation goes to all the bother of preparation — and they don't come.

I remember how St. Vincent Hospital in New York City prepared for massive emergency care after the destruction of the twin towers. But the patients did not come. They could not come. It was too late. Ten men who distorted faith into demonic destruction had seen to that — and surely the God of the three Abrahamic faiths wept. But St. Vincent's heroic effort was not *wasted*.

Neither is a congregation's. We do not know what keeps people from coming. We do not know when they *can't* come for some reason. When they're too timid to come, too deep in hopelessness. When their sense of *life* has been buried by some kind of violence. Our task is to see that they are invited, and that we are prepared to welcome and care for them. Hospitality of the heart puts forth effort as a gift, not a debit card.

The congregation's capacity to create a hospitable space is affected by the condition of its inner life together. As a congregation develops a deep and expansive spiritual life, this spills over into creating an atmosphere that is welcoming and

transformational. The communal outer journey adds breadth.
The communal inner journey adds depth.

In the opening scene of *Chocolat*, the fresh winds of
change blow the church doors open, and the mayor quickly
rises and closes them. Isn't that what we often do? It's risky not
to. Once we open the doors to the winds of the Spirit, no
telling what will happen! Open doors invite change. They offer
hospitality. God's children who have thought themselves to be
orphans may appear in the narthex like unlit candles.

If our congregation is hospitable and flexible enough to
open the doors and extend our beautiful hands, it is our blessed
joy to share the light of Christ's love. We have an opportunity
to offer hospitality of the heart both within and beyond the
community of faith, welcoming those who enter the doors, and
also lifting the feast table and carrying it out into the world.

**To simplify, we subtract.
To stabilize, we add.**

For both individuals
and congregations, simplic-
ity and stability improve
the condition of our interior life. To simplify, we
subtract. To stabilize, we add.
We clutter our cars, clos-
ets, and calendars (personal and
church). We also clutter our souls, like
sand whirling in the wind and blinding us to

the Spirit. We know that we simplify our external lives by clearing out clutter — whether messes, material things, or commitments. We simplify our inner lives by discarding our idols — habits and practices that distract us from facing toward God. Perhaps these idols are an excessive need for praise, power, possessions. They can be whatever we grasp for or falsely place our confidence in or escape to in despair. Freeing ourselves of external and internal clutter, both as persons and as a community of faith, is a matter of radical removal.

Just as we subtract in order to simplify, we add in order to stabilize. Ashworth tells us that steep slopes are complex and highly unstable, and geologists have learned that planting vegetation helps to stabilize them. He says, "If you increase the complexity by adding life, you actually reduce the instability. The more complex, the more stable."[6] Adding life works not only for slopes but also for people.

We feel so overwhelmed with all the complexities of today's world that we don't want to *add* anything. Finding time for spiritual growth increases the complexity of our personal lives. Yet, if we dare to add *life* to our inner space, we reduce our instability — for we sow seeds that produce the fruits of the Spirit and give us faith, meaning, and purpose. Just as emptying the clutter (subtracting) simplifies our lives, so enhancing our depth and expansiveness (adding) stabilizes our lives.

In my observation this also holds for congregations. Narrow faith results in narrow views that ignore God's magnificent complex periphery, and this ignorance (ignore-ance) produces a false stability that in itself is destabilizing and fruitless. In both personal and congregational life, "the more complex, the more stable." We sense this, but we may feel threatened by it. Besides, it smacks of the illogical — like releasing the brakes in a skid. Or taking the leap of faith in a God beyond our comprehension. It's a mystery!

We are given the gift of life, and with that gift comes the mystery of God's divine love.

We who are vulnerable and fallible are entrusted with the amazing opportunity to share that love. To share it in small ways and sacrificial ways. To share it wherever we happen to be — like shuffling through papers with arthritic fingers, offering beautiful hands in hospitality of the heart to someone different, someone new, someone who wouldn't otherwise know what to do.

Chapter Five:

Did You Get Candy?

Thou has given so much to me . . .
Give one thing more — a grateful heart.
— George Herbert

This pleasant day of October 31 at St. Joseph Abbey is a very important one for the Benedictines. It is Hallowed Eve, the eve of All Saints Day in the Christian faith — reduced in the secular world to well-marketed Halloween masks and costumes, "trick or treat" and tummy aches. One of the monks carves jack-o'-lanterns, making visible the capacity of the sacred to enfold the secular. The pumpkins offer hospitality at both the community and guest dining rooms, including me in the fun even though I'm the only guest. A candle glows behind the triangle nose and eyes of the jack-o'-lanterns, and their jagged smiles greet me as I enter.

I eat alone, reflecting on many things. Primarily, how it is with my soul. I eat fast. Too fast. As usual. Because of this, I learn later, I miss a dinner visit from the abbot.

And I also miss something else. On my way to evening prayers I see a young novice who has sometimes served my meals. He has blond hair, a broad smile, and joyful blue eyes. With an excited voice, he asks, "Did you get candy?"

This was the fifth lesson I learned about hospitality of the heart from the Benedictines: Hospitality can transform the ordinary into the extraordinary. The common becomes a source of celebration and joy. New meaning breaks into the mundane.

LESSON 5: Hospitality can transform the ordinary into the extraordinary.

Did you get candy?

When we think of candy in terms of hospitality of the heart, it takes many forms. It can be a gift of our hospitable God — an ordinary/extraordinary gift from nature or from a meaningful moment with one of God's children. Brother David Steindl-Rast, a Benedictine who holds a Ph.D. in experimental psychology, says, "The given is always at hand, in any given situation in this given world; fullness of response to this gift is the goal; what needs to be improved by practice is our response." He goes on to say: "Every night I note in a pocket calendar one thing for which I have never before been consciously thankful. Do you think it is difficult to find a new reason for gratitude every day? Not just one, but three and four and five pop into my mind, some evenings."[1] He has done this for years. I decided to try it. What an incredible experience! During my first year, 365 gifts appeared. (Not a single one related to money or achievement.) Now I'm in my second year and they are still coming. Every day! Each one different!

God's daily gift is here for us. All we have to do is unwrap it, so to speak, to notice it. To stay attuned to those subtle opportunities to be surprised by joy. We recall Jesus' words: *Do you have eyes and fail to see? Do you have ears, and fail to hear?*

And do you not remember? (Mk. 8:18). I used to, as Joan Chittister puts it so well: "miss jonquils in spring and stars at night and the laughter of the children next door."[2] I still do. But I'm more likely to pay attention, to see, and to hear. And to remember. And be grateful.

Being awake to God's daily gifts uplifts us with a sense of anticipation and childlike curiosity. What will be God's gift today? And, sure enough, it comes! Noting the gift helps us realize that God is not silent or invisible. We stop waiting for the burning bush and begin to listen for God in the sounds of nature and the words of others. The common becomes a source of celebration and joy. Ashworth writes that "joy is truly a need . . . Pleasure is intense but shallow; happiness is a moving target which never holds still long enough to reach it. Desire is a social disease. But without joy we die."[3] God created us not only with the capacity for joy but also with the need for it.

God's daily gift is here for us. All we have to do is unwrap it.

Yet, just as I missed candy at the abbey, we miss the ordinary/extraordinary gifts of God's daily hospitality. Oftentimes for the same reason I did — we're in too big a hurry. Or like programmed robots, we're blindly following our habits, and one day's monotony blurs dully into the next, gift unseen. Or we overlook the "candy" given simply because we were expecting something else.

Sometimes we glimpse the gift but miss the joy. We want a different kind of candy. Or a bigger piece. Or we envy someone else whose candy looks better to us. Or we have a sense of entitlement. Envy and entitlement are on the "Top Ten Wanted List" for joy-killers. They produce a habitual shortage of gratitude. Missing joy is a choice. It is a way of declining God's hospitality.

Sometimes we glimpse the gift but miss the joy.

One evening last summer I huddled with my three grandchildren, all of us wrapped together in a shared blanket. We sat on a concrete bench in the amphitheater of the Great Sand Dunes near Alamosa, Colorado. (That in itself — snuggled with my grandchildren — was gift enough.) Both young and old in the crowd listened silently, fascinated by the presentation on lightning by the summer national park ranger — who happened to be my son Dirk. I felt so proud of him. (Another gift.) When it ended and the people left, we walked toward the car with his youngest child Graham now asleep in his arms. The utterly black clear night with its dome full of stars wrapped us in a cosmic miracle. We turned off the flashlight, and Dirk pointed out the constellations and showed us Mars. (Still another gift.) We drove home along the narrow country road surrounded by mountains, and suddenly Dirk braked. A bear! A beautiful bear lumbered into the road, and we watched it come toward us, pass beside us, and turn off into a field. (Gift upon gift! Joy upon joy! Gratitude upon gratitude!)

The words of W. Paul Jones, in *The Province Beyond the River,* come to mind: "Somehow the beauty of this place — it can only be enjoyed. And can it be that through us, God enjoys? It is as if through such joy that creation comes to know itself, and in so knowing knows God."[4] Could Jones be right? Could it be that God enjoys through us? That when we notice the gift and feel the joy and thank the Giver, our Host enjoys the giving? It's a mystery!

Did you get candy?

Getting candy on Halloween or anytime is taken for granted by many of us. It's mundane. But in a monastery setting, getting candy is unexpected, a special surprise. "Candy" — in whatever form — is a means of hospitality, and through it new meaning breaks into the mundane.

My mind goes back in time to the hard Russian winter of 1991 during the transition of the U.S.S.R. into the C.I.S. I recall a bedfast young woman in Ekaterinburg, who received one of the care packages sent by Louisiana United Methodists. When she discovered the Hershey bar, her face beamed with delight, and she spoke that universal word of pleasure, "Ahhhhh!" Getting candy brought joy to her difficult and restricted life.

> We get so much "candy" it's hard not to take the sweet life for granted.

Both the young Russian woman and the young Benedictine brother delighted in getting candy. Yet, there is a major difference. Her life situation of deprivation forces her to live simply. The young brother *chooses* to live simply. The lifestyles of those two young people are so different from mine. My life offers me so much "candy" that the problem is trying not to devour all that is set before me. In fact, I — and probably you too — get so much "candy" it's hard not to take the sweet life for granted.

Let's remember back to when we were children trick-or-treating on Halloween night. We didn't associate it with hospitality or appreciate all those hosts who opened their doors to masked strangers. We didn't consider what was *enough* candy for us, or whether there would be any left for those who came later. No matter how much we received, we kept going door to door asking for more. We got *wa-a-ay* too much candy. Then we had a problem of what to do with it all. Sometimes we hoarded it, Scrooge embodied, possessively protecting it until we ultimately threw out the stale and wasted remainder. Sometimes we overindulged and got sick.

You know where I'm going with this. You see the analogy of our "candy" today. Many of us have more than our share of the world's "candy" — whether we speak of it concretely or abstractly. We still don't reflect on what is *enough* and how our greed affects others. No matter how much we receive, we still want more. And too much candy still leads to problems. If we hoard it, we have to protect it until it's no longer useful or someone inherits it. If we overindulge, we still get sick — sick of soul. But there's another choice. Those of us who take the sweet life for granted are asked a new question, one related to our own hospitality: Did you *give* "candy"?

We are blessed by what we receive, and we are blessed by what we give. Giving a daily gift — a small act of kindness, for example — has similar dynamics to receiving a daily gift. It invites us to pay attention to opportunities to offer hospitality at surprising times and places, to give little gifts in the moment. We discover the joy of giving "candy" away. New meaning breaks into our mundane daily routines.

Each of us has gifts to share, perhaps without realizing it. I recall a note from a stranger who wrote to me about my novel *Crested Butte*. She commented on how Vini (the main character) had used her simple gift to make so much difference around her. "It showed me," wrote the stranger, "that I too have simple gifts I can use for others." It is easy for us to overlook our simple gifts and our small opportunities to offer them. Perhaps we're waiting for the big chance and the dramatic moment, and we miss those common daily opportunities for hospitality. Or the timing is inconvenient, and we procrastinate until the gift is no longer relevant. Or we devalue ourselves: I have no "candy" to give. But everyone does. Everyone! Even in dire situations.

I think of some Russian prisoners who have become United Methodists. With the chaplain's permission and support, they gave the long-lasting gift of building a chapel at the prison. They also give the monthly gift of a musical performance, lively and fun, celebrating that month's birthdays for the prisoners. I happened to be there for the June birthdays. Despite their circumstances, they gave joy to their fellow prisoners and to me. Wherever we are and whatever our situation, we can give "candy." It's a matter of choice.

Hospitality of the heart invites an attitude of detachment toward posses- sions. It relinquishes taking for care-taking. It rises above greed, fair-share side glances, and concerns about guarding turf and getting credit.

Hospitality relinquishes taking for care-taking.

The desert fathers tell about two old men who had lived together for many years without a quarrel:

> The first said, "Let us have one quarrel with each other, as is the way of men."
>
> The other answered, "I do not know how a quarrel happens."
>
> "Look," said the first, "I put a tile between us and say, 'That's mine.' Then you say, 'No, it's mine.' That is how you begin a quarrel."
>
> So they put a tile between them, and the first said, "That's mine."
>
> "No," said the other, "it's mine."
>
> "Yes, it is yours," said the first. "Take it away."
> And they were unable to argue with each other.[5]

Families, friendships, business partnerships, congregations, and communities have been torn asunder because of competition over "candy." It is a choice.

This summer Bill and I worshipped at a church in Madrid, Spain, and I learned their custom regarding birthday gifts.

Instead of *receiving* gifts each birthday, they *give* them. They do this as an expression of gratefulness to God for another year of life. We receive "candy" with gratitude to God, and we give "candy" in grateful response to God for our gifts and also for our continuing life and for God's continual love. Getting candy and giving candy — so ordinary and yet so extraordinary, so commonplace and yet so celebrative.

Did you get candy?

Not everyone does, you know. The human situation is just that — human. It isn't divine. And it isn't always fair. Not all God's children get candy. "Candy" can be something as simple as a peppermint or as elusive as peace. It can take the form of material goods, educational opportunities, social advantages, or political justice. For much of the earth's population, all the chocolate boxes are the same — empty. That's one of the reasons it's so important for those of us who take the sweet life for granted to share our chocolates.

Not all God's children get candy.

George Bernard Shaw said, "This is the true joy in life, the being used for a purpose recognized by yourself as a mighty one; the being thoroughly worn out before you are thrown on the scrap heap; the being a force of nature instead of a feverish selfish little clod of ailments and grievances complaining that the world will not devote itself to making you happy."[6] We have a joyful and life-changing opportunity and responsibility to offer hospitality of the heart to those who don't get "candy."

My friend Mary told me about a mission experience in the Democratic Republic of Congo. She was volunteering outside in a village, giving clothing to the children and serving them food. The children swarmed around them, eager to get the one shirt per child, the one bowl of food. As Mary told me the story, her eyes began to tear. "We ran out of food before we ran out of children." There were fifty hungry children left. And then the village nurse took her inside a makeshift hospital — a large room with over a hundred sick children. And there was nothing left for them.

These African children, like so many, don't get "candy."

During Advent of 2000, I was part of an ecumenical delegation of church leaders who went to the Middle East on a peace fact-finding mission. I was so clear about where I stood on the Israeli-Palestinian conflict that I didn't even bother to think about it. As long as I can remember I have passionately honored the Jewish faith and those who practice it. I was a child when the State of Israel was born, and because of the Holocaust I felt sure that Israelis, knowing what it is to suffer as a people, would never cause another people to suffer. I saw their enemy as my enemy, too. Though I am aware of the damage and fallacies of generalizations and prejudice, I stereotyped the Palestinians — without even realizing it. The word "Palestinian" (to be shamefully honest) automatically conjured in my mind a "terrorist" image. The itinerary called for meetings with several Israeli and Palestinian officials, as well as rabbis, Muslim leaders, and Palestinian Christians. But when I boarded the plane for the Middle East, I felt sure about the facts in advance of the fact-finding mission.

The first hairline crack in my stereotype came when I met with Palestinian Christians. Some of them can trace their family's Christian heritage, unbroken, back to the first century (Father Elias Chacour, for example, the author of *Blood Brothers*).

We tend to forget this. An incident at a civic club in a Texas city offers an illustration. Recently a visiting Palestinian Christian spoke at the monthly meeting. Afterward he answered questions from the audience. "When did you become a Christian?" asked a businessman smugly, an old-timer in the faith. The guest responded with gentle humility, "My family converted about 1500 years ago."

The Palestinian Christians and their ancestors have always walked where Jesus walked. They have always known firsthand the natural landmarks about which he talked. Even their language is similar to the one he spoke. Our biblical translations are based on Hebrew and Greek, and we tend to forget that Jesus (though he would have known temple Hebrew) told his stories and proclaimed the Good News in the common cultural language of Aramaic, the root language of Arabic. These Christians — fruit of the first geographical roots of our faith — are *Palestinians*. But certainly not *terrorists*.

The crack in my stereotype spread while in Bethlehem. We met with the Palestinian mayors of three towns in the Bethlehem District, made up primarily of Christians. All the mayors were Christians. They spoke of the plight of their people: loss of job opportunities, shortage of water, destruction of infrastructure, protection from missiles, powerlessness and hopelessness. That same day I walked past a bulldozed Palestinian Christian business — rebuilt only to be bulldozed again by the Israeli military. Three times. It will not be rebuilt. There is no more money. The Palestinian Christians find themselves to be strangers in their own land, shown hostility rather than hospitality.

My stereotype shattered totally the afternoon I stood with a Palestinian Christian grandmother and mother and baby in the rubble of their home in Beit Jolla. A home housing three generations. A home built by the grandfather, each stone and arch and window lovingly placed over a period of twenty-five years. A home destroyed by the Israeli military in a few minutes. Amidst the ruins I saw three missiles that said "USA."

Later I saw a USA missile that had destroyed part of a Christian hospital. During our fact-finding mission, a Palestinian Catholic seminary was fired on by the Israeli military for half an hour. Later a Christian orphanage was stormed and held for several days. Before me now on my desk, as I write this, is a fragment of blue window glass I picked up from the debris of a Christian youth center. Beside the glass is a remnant from shattered roof tiles that I found in the children's playground of a Christian church. These bits of debris witness to missiles unleashed on innocent Christians who have no weapons, are not terrorists, have never harbored terrorists, are not part of any terrorist organization, and have no terrorist link. Our missiles inflicted on the innocent!

My taxes. My guilt. My shame. And my sorrow, my deep sorrow that spills over in silent tears, for this injustice runs counter to the spirit of our great country.

The followers of Jesus are innocent victims — in the *Holy Land* of all places! And they are rapidly declining in this land where Jesus lived — down from 50 percent in this area half a century ago to less than 2 percent today. How can we even conceive of the Holy Land without Christians! Yet how can they remain without support? One soft-spoken Palestinian man asked with deep puzzlement, "Where are the Christians of the world? Why aren't they supporting us?" The three Abrahamic faiths — Judaism, Christianity, and Islam — share the same Middle East roots. The Arab world supports the Palestinian Muslims, and our country supports Israel. The Palestinian Christians have no advocate. They stand alone, expendable to both sides. *Where are the Christians?*

The Palestinian Christians don't get "candy."

I withdrew the Christians from my stereotype of Palestinians as terrorists. But what about the rest of them? What about the people in Gaza? (Mine was a deeply entrenched prejudice. Prejudice and hospitality of the heart cannot coexist.)

Prejudice and hospitality of the heart cannot coexist.

The Gaza memory that stands out to me the most is the half-block of debris from three Palestinian homes in the countryside.

These Muslim families were suddenly awakened in the middle of the night by Israeli soldiers pounding on their doors and shouting a five-minute warning to get out. Then their houses were bulldozed along with everything in them. All that they owned was demolished — beds and linens, tables and dishes, books and TV, cookware and clothing, toys and family mementoes. Some items scattered among the piles of debris stood out to me. A little black shoe. A twisted stroller. A broken doll. I picked up a school workbook half-buried, and with the father's permission I tore out a page. Words ran across it, followed by blank lines to practice those beautiful confusing letters of Arabic. I walked with six of the children beside the rubble that had been their homes. We communicated through our gestures, smiles, and eyes. The page from the schoolbook belonged to one of those precious homeless children. That mangled page is also before me now on my desk. I asked an American friend who is fluent in Arabic to translate it for me. The writing exercise from their Gaza school was about loving others.

These Palestinian children, like so many, don't get "candy."

And neither do the Israeli children. They live with the fear of a terrorist attack. When the random innocent are targeted, mass fear and desire for revenge is a common response. That tragic Tuesday of 2001 prompted the same response in our country: Do whatever is necessary to stop terrorists! (In response, however, our military took great care to limit its target to *terrorists* and to protect innocents from harm.)

Shirley, my dear friend for three decades, is Jewish. Her daughter married a rabbi, moved to Jerusalem, and had six children. Now, they live in a beautiful home in one of the

Israeli settlements in Palestinian Territory in the West Bank. While in the Middle East, I visited with her. She talked about her children and about how green and lush everything is in her settlement. She told me, showing courage, that she feels safe except for an occasional sniper. I'm very grateful for her well-being. She is my friend, and I care deeply for her mother. I pray that Shirley's daughter and grandchildren will always be safe.

At one of the delegation meetings I met a new friend, a rabbi in Jerusalem. Young men and women are required to serve a term in the Israeli army, and his daughter is currently serving. Each morning when she leaves home, he shudders in the shadow of uncertainty about her safe return. His head understands the Palestinians' concerns about Israeli settle-ments in their territory, poverty-inducing restrictions, and displaced refugees. But his heart supports disproportionate force against the Palestinians. He wants his daughter to be safe — I do, too.

Both Israeli and Palestinian children are caught in the crossfire of the Israeli cry for security from terrorism and the Palestinian cry for freedom. Perhaps that is partly why the Palestinian people have pleaded for so many years to have international peacekeepers in the area. History has shown that there are times for a just war to force peace. But forced peace must be a peace with justice. Otherwise, the volatility caused by loss of land and life and hope boils beneath the surface and erupts in sporadic volcanoes or seeps into streams that eventually flow into the main rivers. And the grassroots fathers and mothers and children on both sides pay a horrific price.

My stereotype of Palestinians is belatedly gone. This experience taught me that prejudices influence us regarding who deserves "candy." They give us permission to set certain people outside the hospitality of our hearts. We do this as individual Christians, and we also do it collectively as congregations.

Prejudices influence us regarding who deserves "candy."

We are responsible for our own prejudices. But why are they so deep? Why are they so unconscious sometimes? We aren't born with them, so where do we learn them? From family? Friends? Culture? Fiction? Nonfiction?

Writing is subjective; and, whether consciously or unconsciously, the writer's perceptions sneak into the work, including nonfiction. The same holds for "objective reporting." It's an oxymoron. Subconscious stereotypes, perceptions, and prejudices can shade even the sharpest news reporter's interpretations. The stories told, photographs shown, and words used are all choices, and these choices sway the audience's perceptions of the "facts." For example, sometimes the choice is made to limit a death report to the number killed — no names, no stories about the victims, no pictures. Merely a statistic to lodge in our heads. Sometimes, however, the choice is made to include the name, a human interest story, and a sympathy-inducing photograph — and emotions are aroused. The heart is touched. A fellow human being has died. We are saddened. Perhaps angry.

Cumulative stories can slant toward a particular vantage point (unintentionally or perhaps in consideration of marketing and financial consequences). On the conscious level we as the audience probably don't even notice what is happening. But language is powerful, and over time our political perceptions can be subconsciously shaped: This group deserves "candy." That group does not.

The sunrise is very important to me. During the writing of *Through the East Window*, I began to see the sunrise as a symbol of hope in the midst of loss. No matter where I am, I look for it each morning, and I have often pondered what God is saying through it. In relation to hospitality of the heart, I have a clue.

"Candy" is intended for all God's people.

The sunrise is offered daily to everyone in every part of the world. It isn't dependent on affluence or advantages. It isn't based on a judgment of who deserves it and who doesn't. No one is excluded. For me, the daily sunrise shows us one of God's dreams: "Candy" in both its visible and invisible forms is intended for all God's people.

"Did you get candy?" the young brother asks me.
Ahh! Indeed so! Indeed so!
Then comes a cosmic whisper: "Did you *give* candy?"

CHAPTER SIX:

One Strand
of Web

All are parts of one stupendous whole.
— Alexander Pope

I return from breakfast, sit down at the desk, and re-read what I wrote in my journal on my first morning at the abbey:

> I come here disheveled, seeking wholeness,
> seeking not to distract myself from soulfulness, giv-
> ing logic and will a rest, bowing to the yearnings of
> my soul, my deepest truest self.

More words form in my mind and fall on the page. More thoughts. More insights. I check my watch and put down the pen. It is time.

I close the door to my room and begin the slow-motion walk to the chapel. For many years I've wanted to take this step. Perhaps, more accurately, it is not so much a step as a bowing, a silent internal bowing of my life before the Loving Holy One. With feelings too deep for words, I stand at the center altar continuing my faith journey, but from a new starting place. I will leave the chapel an Oblate Novice of St. Benedict affiliated with St. Joseph Abbey.

Father Dominic is ready. His mellifluent voice reads the words of the ceremony. One part especially touches my soul. It has to do with being ready to:

> give generously of yourself to the building up of true
> Christian fellowship with those around you: the

strong and the weak, the wise and the unwise, the healthy and the sick, the rich and the poor, the joyous and those afflicted with misery and sorrow, the lovable and the unlovable, the secure and the insecure, those well cared for and those who are neglected, the young and the aged, those placed over you and those who are under your care, those of your faith and those not of your faith, whether in affairs of Church, business, government, or any other area of life.[1]

There is no fine-print disclaimer — no *if* (they meet my prerequisites), no *except* (for "river rats"), no *until* (they do something "wrong"). There is no wiggle room for uplifting one group of humanity by trodding on another — no dividing into camps, no pitting one side against the other, no polarization. Paul put it this way: *There is no longer Greek and Jew, circumcised and uncircumcised, barbarian, Scythian, slave and free, but Christ is all and in all!* (Col. 3:9-11)

Finally, *finally,* with humility and gratitude I offer my life in a new way. That is what *oblate* means — to offer. This sacred ceremony changes nothing — and, yet, it changes everything. Though nothing in my outer life is different, this moment is a continual lifelong reminder to be attuned to the Rule of St. Benedict and attempt to live it out in the world, to try to enact the multidimensional hospitality of the heart that is entailed in following the Christ — knowing that I will fail daily. This new journey is primarily about my inner life, and my heart overflows with gratitude and joy. For the moment at least, my inner space deepens and becomes more expansive, like a calm sea at sunrise. This oblation — this offering of myself — is a symbolic acceptance of God's invitation to be one with God and all God's creation. An invitation that gently but deeply calls me to unfold from God's little bud to God's faithful flower, one petal at a time.

After I leave Father Dominic, I take a long walk alone. It is so still I can hear the autumn leaves land softly on the lane. I savor watching them float down, miniature pieces of a gold-to-red rainbow. I notice a leaf ahead of me that is suspended in space. It flutters at eye level, gently blowing from side to side, but not falling. It's a mystery!

As I come closer, the sun catches a single thread of spider web. It glints in the light, and I see that it is holding the leaf. My eyes follow it upward, higher and higher to its place of beginning on the branch of a tall pine tree far above me. The leaf dangles, free to flutter as it will, yet held securely. I stand before it, released from hurry and distractions, savoring the moment and pondering the possibilities of its meaning. What might God say through a fluttering leaf hanging from one strand of web that catches the sunlight?

As I watched and reflected, wrapped in a sense of peace on these Benedictine holy grounds, I learned my sixth lesson about hospitality of the heart: God's cosmic hospitality holds us all and connects us together.

LESSON 6: God's cosmic hospitality holds us all and connects us together.

God holds each individual leaf and the entire tree of humankind, every single branch. As individuals and communities we flutter and whirl through times of celebration and crisis, abundance and abasement. Nature brings disasters upon us. Nations bring disasters upon each other. We blow one another about — and up. But through it all, God holds us securely. We are connected, to borrow Ashworth's words, "on a small, blue planet spinning around a medium-sized, class-G star."² We dangle together from one strand of web.

We are connected to our homeland earth. Creation itself witnesses to God's cosmic hospitality. All God's creatures share the poetry of sun and soil, air and water. When we were a rural society, we had daily reminders of cosmic hospitality. We *knew* that we stood barefoot on holy ground. Our generous hospitable God created a wonderful — wonder-filled — earth for us. Psalm 104 describes it well:

> *God, my God, how great you are! . . .*
> *You set earth on a firm foundation*
> *so that nothing can shake it, ever . . .*
> *You started the springs and rivers,*
> *sent them flowing among the hills.*
> *All the wild animals now drink their fill, . . .*
> *You water the mountains from your heavenly cisterns; . . .*
> *You make grass grow for the livestock,*
> *hay for the animals that plow the ground . . .*
> *The moon keeps track of the seasons,*
> *the sun is in charge of each day . . .*

> *Meanwhile, men and women go out to work,*
> *busy at their jobs until evening.*
> *What a wildly wonderful world, God!*

Through this wildly wonderful world, God invites us to come close, to live in communion with Creator and creation, life with life, plucking our individual notes in the colossal concerto of the cosmos.

Some places on God's earth are special to us. They are sanctuaries, places of contemplation and holiness that offer us refuge and tranquility. A special place may be a specific spot in nature or in a church or a space set aside in the home. As a child, I used to climb up on my swinging trapeze and safely ponder my small realm, both the outer and the inner. Bill grew up on a farm, and his special childhood place was the river bottom where he ran in the sand or reflected on the waves. A place sacred to both of us now is the top of a ridge in the Colorado Rockies that offers a panoramic view of God's mountains and lakes — where I now climb to contemplate my inner and outer worlds. Periodically (as when I arrived at the abbey), we need the hospitality of special places where we can go disheveled, seeking wholeness, giving logic and will a rest, where we can bow to the yearnings of our souls.

When we experience connection with a special place, grand or simple, we connect with God.

When we experience connection with a special place, grand or simple, we connect with God. We feel the Spirit. Our disheveled minds and hurried bodies merge with our souls once more. Our sense of struggle for the essentials of living eases, and we savor the essence of life. We become mindful guests aware of the presence of the Host.

Has a guest you were hosting ever accidentally broken a glass or stained a rug? Of course. It happens, and it's insignificant. But what if a guest deliberately tossed a bent spoon in the trash or dumped coffee on the carpet? Or took most of the pie instead of merely a piece? Or stole an heirloom goblet? Or ripped a hole in the napkin covering the bread? Or filled the air with cigar smoke? Or spit in the water pitcher? That's disgusting! Guests don't behave that way.

Or do we? Our gracious and generous Host has opened the table to greedy and careless guests. Don't we pollute our water and air, rip holes in the ozone, snatch our heirloom minerals? Burke's novel *Bitterroot* includes a debate about the environment, and one character expresses a common notion: "The Earth was put here for a purpose, to nurture and sustain us. The minerals we take from the ground are like the vegetables we grow on our farms. They're all gifts from the Lord." Gifts, yes. But only the vegetables are replaceable.

And as God's guests in the West, don't we take more than our share of the world's limited resources? Don't we stain the green carpet of landscape with clear cutting and logging roads? Don't we practice nix-it-don't-fix-it consumerism, getting rid of whatever is bent and torn? That would have been unimaginable to Abba Mius:

When a soldier asked him about repentance, Abba Mius responded, "Tell me, if your cloak is torn, do you throw it away?"

The soldier replied that he mends it and uses it again.

Abba Mius asked, "If you are so careful about your cloak, will not God be equally careful about his creature?"[3]

The good abba could not use that simile effectively today, for the skill of mending has been lost to the ease of spending. Lucky for us that God isn't a throwaway God! We are like old darned socks, ever patched, never tossed.

> **Unavoidable natural and logical consequences result when we let reasonable need be twisted by greed.**

To abuse God's cosmic hospitality and grace is to stuff a secret deep down in the stocking toe. This secret is something we know but pretend not to know. Ashworth dares to reach down and pull it out, setting it before us in bold neon lights: Human beings "have never eradicated a single law of nature nor escaped its consequences."[4] Despite our game of pretend, unavoidable natural and logical consequences result when God's grabby guests let reasonable need be twisted by greed. While we run headlong toward the consequences of our actions, God still holds us securely by one strand of web — but it is a link that offers us unconditional love, not protection from ourselves. When a species takes on nature, ultimately nature prevails. (Ask the dinosaurs.)

Ashworth suggests that Earth has been evolving for four billion years and has twelve billion years remaining.[5] To simplify our grasp of this concept, let's think of a person with a life expectancy of a century who is now twenty-five. God's earthlings have not been around since the beginning, but let's assume we are in early adulthood. We are youthful and filled with dreams, eager to conquer and reticent to cherish. And we know less than we think we do. We presume our soundbyte bank of information passes for knowledge. We lack the experience needed for wisdom. We are impatient and crowd out time for reflection, discarding opportunities to draw wisdom from the little experience we have.

In our arrogance we overlook mystery and reverence. We forget to bow to the Creator. John Killinger says, "Bowing is a wonderful way of expressing our humanity, our sense of reverence for the Creator and the creation."[6] How often we skip through God's "wildly wonderful world" without pausing to bow!

We also forget to bow to each other. Killinger speaks of bowing as "the spirit of acceptance, compliance, humility, deference." That is not the kind of spirit we're taught in business school. Or law school. Or journalism. Or marketing. Or politics. It sounds anti-American! We are *not* a passive people. And I celebrate that. I don't think God expects us to be. Jesus was not passive! But Jesus connected — to God, to nature, to the disciples, to the crowds. And Jesus bowed. He declined all temptations to be "Number One." He invites us also to bow.

Abba Apollo affirmed bowing when receiving others: "Not that we bow down before them, but before God who is in them."[7] Bowing is not a gesture of false subservience to others, but a reminder of faithful servanthood to God through honoring them. In some cultures bowing, or a nod of the head with folded hands, is still the proper greeting. Perhaps even in our own hand-shaking society, practicing hospitality of the heart leads to receiving others with an invisible bow, an inner nod toward kindly perceptions of them, charitable interpretations of their behavior, and cordial reactions to them. Bowing, whether an outer or inner gesture, recognizes connection.

It is ironic that we *are* connected, but we don't *connect.* Yet, to do so benefits us physically as well as emotionally and spiritually. In his book entitled *Connect,* Edward Hallowell lists a dozen vital ties: family of origin (parents and siblings); immediate family (family we create); friends and community; work, mission, activity (including a goal or hobby); beauty (art, music, literature); the past (an awareness of where we came from rather than assuming time began when we were born); nature and special places; pets and other animals; ideas and information (the pleasure of thought, of evolving philosophies); institutions and organizations; whatever is beyond knowledge (God), and the self.[8] These connections

> **It is ironic that we are connected, but we don't connect.**

open our hearts and deepen our souls. Hallowell cites research demonstrating that they also lengthen our lives. Birth, of course, is ultimately fatal. But when we *connect*, we are apt to live longer. More important, we're *alive* while we live.

In *The Man Who Killed the Deer*, Waters depicts a meeting of the tribal council, "There was faith and doubt, orthodoxy and heresy, wisdom and folly, the conservatism of age and the impetuousness of youth. There was trouble." There often is in human relations — including those in congregations. We don't live in harmony with our connectedness. We prefer selective connection. We drain our energy in the destructive delusion that we can lop off part of God's creation (or part of the congregation), as though we don't all dangle from one strand of web. The "old men" of the tribal council listened to everyone before speaking, and then they said, "Let us move evenly together." What a lot of pain that simple approach would save! But, of course, we don't have time to listen to *everyone*. And moving evenly together is inefficient. And it leaves little plotting room for pushing through one's own agenda. And it might break the Eleventh Commandment: Thou shalt not go past adjournment time! We're busy. We have to move on to the next trouble and the next. Trouble perhaps caused by failing to recognize that we are connected and, therefore, actions and words have a ripple effect. Trouble perhaps prevented by taking the time to listen and the effort to "move evenly together."

We have a long way to go in learning how to bow and how to move evenly together and also how to forgive. God is so generous in forgiveness of us; yet, we are so stingy in forgiveness of others. Forgiveness has a crucial role in healing our rampant disease of disconnectedness.

We are not talking about the cliché to forgive and forget. We are talking about the challenge to remember and forgive. Forgiving is not the partner of forgetting. True forgiveness is married to remembering. Some things *shouldn't* be forgotten, like the Jewish Holocaust and the earlier Armenian Holocaust. Some things *can't* be forgotten. Palestinians can't forget their loss of loved ones and land and olive groves due to Israeli militarism — just as Israelis can't forget their loss of loved ones due to Palestinian terrorism. The Middle East conflict is a bloody portrayal of a human truth: Whatever the situation, a response of hatred is destructive. The conflict on that small piece of land (with extremists on both sides engaging in provocation and sabotaging peace) is a living lesson about what happens when forgiveness is replaced by revenge in the vocabulary of the heart.

Whatever the situation, a response of hatred is destructive.

I think of an Israeli girl who celebrated her twelfth birthday the same week my granddaughter did. But her party became a terrorist target. She and her family had not participated in wounding and killing Palestinians. They had not demolished Palestinian homes and businesses. They had not destroyed ancient olive groves. They were having a *party*. What kind of person targets the innocent? How can her family forgive?

I think of a boy five years older and an event three months before. An Orthodox Christian, he often sat at the entrance to the Church of the Nativity in Bethlehem and handed out scarves to women who wished to cover their heads in respect for Orthodox tradition. On this day he came out of the church from worship with his family. He was carrying the baby of one of his cousins, trying to make him laugh. At that moment a shot rang out from an Israeli sniper, hitting the boy. He gently lay the baby down on the stones of Manger Square and then fell over dead. He was not on a "wanted" list. He was a Christian coming from worship in the church we associate with the birth of our Lord. What kind of person targets the innocent? And what kind of person shoots at someone holding a baby? How can his family forgive?

Yet, healing comes when we remember and forgive. I have heard Palestinian Christians, who could have fanned passion, say instead, "We must always remember to have compassion for Israelis as well as Palestinians." And I have seen Israeli Jews protest the treatment of Palestinians. These are the ones on both sides who are healed of hatred, who have journeyed from passion to compassion.

Healing comes when we remember and forgive.

Passion that blinds us to compassion is human, under-standable, and common. But it is not of God. Forgiveness is of God. People who remember and forgive witness to God's empowering love and grace, and the power of their witness brings hope and courage to those around them. Forgiving is part of the essence of the Christian faith — forgiving even though we remember things that justify harboring a desire for revenge. Forgiveness does not necessarily change our bit of the world, but it does redefine our own view of it, and that in itself can change our response.

Families can become dysfunctional because members will not forgive each other. Likewise, a lack of forgiveness among members and groups in a church can lead to a dysfunctional congregation that operates in the name of Christ but not in the spirit of Christ. Jesus said, *Blessed are the peacemakers, for they will be called children of God* (Mt. 5:9). A version based on Aramaic, the language Jesus would have spoken when he taught the people gathered around him, puts it this way: Blessed are "those who bear the fruit of sympathy and safety for all; they shall hasten the coming of God's new creation."[9] As we offer hospitality of the heart, we do just that. We behave as children of God, bearing the fruit of sympathy and safety for all, practicing the connection that already existed.

All of creation is ever connected and also ever changing. When two planes flew into the magnificent twin towers of New York City and they toppled before our eyes, many messages crowded our minds and hearts. First, disbelief. Then the horror began to seep into our being. We mourned the loss of so many lives. And we felt violated. And we were struck by the amputation of a familiar landmark in the skyline. *Gone!* As I reflected on that change, one message recurred to me, over and over again, like a headline crawling repeatedly across a news board: All things are temporal. *All* things.

We have taken for granted the permanence of our gigantic manmade skylines. Not so! Only God is permanent. And change. Think of the changes to Earth over the eons. The changes in cultures over the ages. The changes in family traditions over the generations. Even the ownership of a prized piece of property is but a moment's lease in the overall scheme.

Ashworth speaks of the "incontrovertible, uncomfortable, fundamental presence of impermanence":

> On our small bit of tumbling mud, with stars and galaxies whirling dizzily around us and even the mud itself shifting beneath our feet, we live our lives as though the universe were static. It is perfectly understandable that we should live this way, but it is wrong . . . Moment follows moment, age follows age; creatures and climates evolve, rivers wear through rock, the endless sea itself ends . . .
>
> Always change.
> Always change.
> All ways change.[10]

We are one together in a dynamic cosmic dance.

Yes. There is always change, and all ways change. We are one together in a dynamic cosmic dance.

We enter the scene in the midst of the drama, without a copy of the script. Our birth is not the beginning, nor our death the finale. We inherit the past but we place our mark on the future. Sometimes indelibly. The heroic firefighters and rescue workers after the twin towers were struck will not be forgotten. Neither will the courageous passengers of the fourth plane: "Let's roll!" Far more often, however, our mark on the future goes unnoticed. Yet, it is there through the ripples of our words and deeds, through the lives we touch, and through our making our small space on earth better at the end of our role in the drama than it was when we entered the scene.

I think of my friend Linda. Loving nature, she would have noticed the leaf dangling from one strand of web even without being on retreat. She said a reverberating *YES!* to life, aware of the permanence of change, but unafraid. At the reception for her husband and her when Tom retired as a pastor, she gave even more hospitality than she received. Her ability to connect with others stood out that night as she spoke in a personal way to each one there — and hundreds were in the receiving line. They came in love and respect. They came in appreciation, for Linda had helped them not only connect with her, but also with each other. Wherever she went, she filled the space of her life with energy and care for others, offering hospitality of the heart to friends and strangers alike. That night was no exception — despite the toll the last stages of bone cancer were taking on her frail and shrunken body. History did not note her passing, but all of us whose lives she touched continue to note it. She left her space on earth better than she found it, and her goodness ripples on through the effect she had on our lives.

All of us in the human family dangle together, ever connected and ever changing. Held securely by one strand of web.

CHAPTER SEVEN:
Leaving Home

Without the still center, the journey, whether inner or outer, is impossible.
— Esther de Waal

*W*orship at the abbey ends. The last service for me. My daily rhythm of praise and routine of solitude are over. It's time to leave. To go back to the airport and catch another plane, this time in the light.

I hurry to the door of the sanctuary, not speaking to anyone. Not even saying goodbye, for tears flood my face. I rush to the car before the dam fully gives way. The key turns. The motor hums. But my tears blur the road, and I can't see to drive. I begin to sob, deep racking sobs.

I've been here so brief a time. Why this overwhelming grief? What is the source? I enjoy and appreciate my normal life. I love my family. I have good friends. I like where we live and feel a sense of purpose and meaning. I'm not here at the abbey to escape from anything. I don't dread returning. So why these sobs? These soul-wrenching sobs.

What is the power of this place?

Many days later, still reflecting on the source of those tears, I talked with my son Bryant on the phone. He asked about the abbey, and I recounted some of my experiences. He listened well as always. Then I admitted my farewell tears and shared my confusion.

After a pause, with that amazing insight he sometimes shows, he said simply, "You were *home*."

The *Aha!* of truth. That was it! I was leaving *home*.

I was leaving the comfort of a community where truth and goodness and peace abide, where humility and service are manifested, and where the bells of praise and worship toll four times a day. Where people are consciously at home with God. Where they are awake to the bounty of sharing bread. Where they do not trod on the beauty of this moment in a race to the next.

To return to the home where I love to be, I had to leave the home where I long to be.

How do we get the two together — the longing for the spiritual and the living in the secular? How do we develop and support our inner life as we go about our outer life? How do we build a portable altar, a sanctuary within ourselves that is so much a part of who we are that we consciously carry a bit of the divine with us in our daily walk in the world? How do we merge body, mind, and soul into an integrated whole?

We do not know the answers. We identify with Martiniano in Waters' novel: *"He did not know. . . . He did not know. But within him he felt something stirring awake. The power within him that knew what he did not know . . . Awake! Awake! Awake!"*

We awake to the space within that is undefiled, undefined by logic, and undivided.

Sometimes something stirs awake within us,

something that parts the drapes to what we already knew. For the moment we awake to the space within that is undefiled, undefined by logic, and undivided from universal oneness in the One. We tingle with aliveness on all levels and through all layers. In those moments, leaving home and going home become one and the same.

Those moments pass. We go to sleep again. And again awaken. Regressing and progressing on our spiritual journey. But for now, in *this* moment, let's be aware of the stirring. *Awake!*

Home is a word with multilevel meanings and images. Human beings have deep needs related to it. We need to know that there is a place we can call home. We need to feel at home in ourselves, with others, and in the world around us. We also need to feel at home with God.

Our need for a place we can call home is not as easily met in our culture today as it was in previous centuries. Recently, a young taxi driver picked me up at the airport. We talked a bit, and I asked the common question, "Where is home for you?"

"I don't know. I'm twenty-four years old, and I've lived in twenty-five countries. I don't know where home is."

He began telling me about his faith journey. He said his parents had been "hippies" in the seventies. "They joined the Jesus Movement, and I grew up a Christian. But I wasn't connected to any church." He told me he knew the Bible well — and why: "Whenever I did something wrong, I had to stand in the corner with my face to the wall and quote Bible verses."

He'd been a missionary in Russia for four years but had recently returned, disillusioned.

"You can't just talk about faith," he said. "You have to experience it." Now he was interested in Zen Buddhism. He called himself a seeker.

He is one of the many homeless who pay their rent.

Home is more than a place. We need to feel at home in ourselves. Otherwise, our lives become littered with unlived-in days. It is interesting that we can be full of ourselves — self-aggrandizing, self-centered, self-demanding — and not be at home in ourselves. We have become accustomed to out-of-body experiences, to being absent from ourselves — to a commuter arrangement, showing up on weekends or perhaps not at all.

We can be full of ourselves and not be at home in ourselves.

We are so "absent-selfed" that we check the clock to see if it is time to be hungry! We may not be in tune with the self, but we are in sync with our gold wristwatch. It counts down each minute, patrolling when we eat and sleep, come and go. One brief alarm beep has the power to change the direction of our feet. We clock in and out, whether or not we're on the clock.

We are more familiar with living *for* some moment than living *in* the moment. For the *now* is lost in the lurch toward some anticipated future moment. Until that moment comes.

And then passes. And the *now* is lost again in the nostalgic backward glance at that past moment. This pattern exacts a heavy price, perpetually eroding the present.

When we feel at home with ourselves, we look at time from a different perspective. We enter into the rippling stream of the present, carried gently forward in the current of the cosmic clock. We know the beauty and wonder of the moment, this unmeasured moment suspended from digital time.

We know the beauty and wonder of the moment.

When we feel at home with ourselves, we are *there* when we offer hospitality to another.

We need to feel at home with others as well as ourselves. In *The Snow Falcon* by Stuart Harrison, the main character is Michael Somers. He introduces himself to Tom, the veterinarian:

> Tom didn't react, though he recognized the name sure enough. He'd known Michael's dad before he died, and he knew that Michael had been to prison and for what, though what he read in the papers he always regarded with a degree of skepticism. He'd heard something about Michael's coming back to town, and the things people were saying. He saw the way Michael was watching him, a little uncertain, maybe a little defiantly, as if he

expected the mention of his name to provoke a particular response.

Tom held out his hand. "Welcome home."

Michael hesitated, then took it. "Thanks," he said, and for the first time since he'd been back, he started to feel as if maybe he really was coming home after all.

During the moments that we feel at home with others, the heartsickness of homesickness is healed.

How simple it is! Hospitality of the heart welcomes people home. It is like a promise. There is a sense of expectancy of something not yet that will be. Brother David says the heart is "where self and all and God are united." It is "the crossroads of the visible and the invisible."[1] When we offer hospitality of the heart, we meet at the crossroads. We share together the deep essence of silent communion that can be neither seen nor heard, but is as real to us as a breath, a life-giving breath.

When we share welcome-home hospitality, the door is ajar to new possibilities. We feast together, awake to the bounty of sharing bread. Our words take on deeper meaning, and we enter into understanding. Our spirits touch. We recognize the unimportance of the importance of image and the insignificance of the significance of position. Sharing

We feast together, awake to the bounty of sharing bread.

hospitality of the heart is a coming home, and we are home as long as the sharing lasts.

We need to feel at home in the world around us. That is not always easy. About the time we get familiar with our world like a comfortable old chair, get our slippers on and our feet up, the world changes. *Again!* When we think about the overwhelming needs in the world, we can begin to feel paralyzed. If we peek out at the culture around us, sometimes we feel shocked by the values portrayed. Perhaps we feel weighed down and betrayed by decisions enacted by our congregation, nation, or denomination — decisions that represent us as part of the group, but that we believe to be wrong and are helpless to change. There may be times when we want to leave its shadows, the menace and madness, and join the sheep who left the flock, and go hide from the ninety and nine. (When that happens, sure enough, the Shepherd comes.)

As we look at the world around us, there are also beautiful moments when we recognize what it is to be at home in the world. To feel our oneness with the global community. Our oneness with Carmichael the polar bear and Tweetie the parakeet. With an ancient bristlecone pine and yellow brown-eyed blossoms that follow the sun. To be part of flood and flame, bread and word, mystery and wonder.

We need to feel at home with God. We want to overcome the scars of stand-in-the corner Bible-verse punishment. We want to trust that grace really can overcome shame. We want to rest in the Oneness. We recognize that quest within ourselves and see it in the faces of people around us.

But how can we be at home with this One we call by lofty names: *Earth-Tamer, Ocean-Pourer, Mountain-Maker, Hill-Dresser* (Ps. 65)? We have accumulated centuries of phrases in our efforts to describe this Holy One of many names who is above all names: *solid rock under my feet, breathing room for my soul . . . granite-strength and safe-harbor God* (Ps. 62). In our feeble attempts to grasp the One beyond grasping, we try to get our minds around personal/transcendent God, imminent/omniscient God, internal/intangible God. And then, weary of words, we fall asleep in the middle of our prayers!

Imagine a mother whose child falls asleep during a bedtime prayer. We can see her bend to stroke the forehead, softly kiss the cheek, then pausing a moment she smiles down tenderly at the sleeping child, her eyes filled with love. So it is, I think, with God, who tenderly enfolds us — even when we fall asleep during our prayers. We simply *are* at home with God. That is our starting place, God's gift to us.

Though we are intrinsically at home with God — though it is our starting place, our gift — it is also the place we seek all our lives. For faith is not bound to logic. It is filled with paradox. Only in rare moments do we recognize with surprise that we are already home. We *awake*!

When we feel at home with God, home is wherever we are. As

When we feel at home with God, home is wherever we are.

Christians, our task is to live the faith in the world. We are
invited to take the goodness we find on consecrated ground
and translate it into everyday living. In the novel *All We
Know of Heaven*, Rémy Rougeau describes Antoine's feelings after pronouncing his vows as a monk: "The emotion
Antoine felt was broader than gratitude. He was apprecia-
tive, yes, but he also wanted to be better than he was: more
virtuous, more sympathetic, more responsible to the world."
We do not have to take vows to know that sense of emotion
Antoine felt. We yearn to be more mature in our faith, to
become the one God created us to be. We yearn to be more
generous toward others, as God is so generous toward us.
We yearn to help move our tiny bit of the world a little
closer to becoming what God created it to be. *Thy kingdom
come! Thy will be done!*

When we feel at home with God, we become so aware of
God's presence in all of life that home can be any place. It isn't
limited to a particular house, a specific place, or a group of people. It can be a palace or a prison. It can be a circle of fire that
one who is homeless shares with another. Home becomes
mobile. It is wherever we carry our inner "table" into the world
and invite others to it. It is wherever we welcome others and
help them feel, as did Michael Sommers, that maybe they really
are coming home after all.

Let us return once more to the abbey. I sat in the guest
refectory for breakfast, my last meal there. I was kindly served,
as always, and then I sat alone as I had for each meal. I sat at
the same place each time, facing the door at a table for four in

the corner. That last morning I dared to let my imagination take me where it would:

Jesus enters. He's here in this room and also sits down to breakfast. But I cannot envision him at my little table, so near to me. He sits at the head of the long table in the center of the room. I recall all the paintings, tapestries, and sculptures that place him at the middle of the table with his disciples on each side. But I can only visualize him at the head.

There he sits this morning! The people at his table are mixed in gender, age, and race. Everyone is glad to be with him. He sees a highchair standing against the wall, rises, and brings it to the table beside him. He lifts a toddler and puts her in the highchair, carefully fastening the safety strap. She smiles up at him, and he smiles back.

He takes the bread, blesses it, and breaks it.

During breakfast he enjoys the fellowship and food and laughs with the people who fill his table. He smiles a lot, nods his head to various ones, and offers words of encouragement.

I watch with pleasure from my place alone, off to the side.

Then unexpectedly I begin to wonder whether he would see me sitting by myself if this were real. He would glance toward me. Wouldn't he?

He's involved with the people at his table. But wouldn't he be aware of everyone in the room? Wouldn't he scan it for those on the edge? Wouldn't he notice one sitting alone? Wouldn't he smile? Nod? Acknowledge that one in some way? Wouldn't he?

Wouldn't he peer discreetly at the people around him? Looking for tears or pain in the eyes? Listening for words of hurt to heal or joy to share? Wouldn't he?

Suddenly it happens! My imagination breaks through all barriers. And He glances my way. He sees me. And from His place at His table, He smiles at me. Even me.

This is the One our hearts seek, the One who is always with us, the One who teaches us to trust in the Presence and invites us to say with our lives: The table is prepared. The Bread is blessed and broken for you. Won't you come? All has been made ready.

Guide for Groups

Hospitality of the Heart lends itself to use by groups. The "Reflections" and the material that follows can be easily adapted for short-term study groups, Sunday school classes, and retreats.

A WORD FOR LEADERS

As leader, your primary tasks are to model hospitality of the heart and set up a hospitable atmosphere. It will be helpful to see yourself as a facilitator rather than a teacher. Questions for reflection and discussion of each chapter can be found in "Reflections" (following this section). These questions are offered as a resource rather than an assignment. You may want to introduce the study with "Getting Started" in "Reflections."

Six suggestions are offered:
- Beginning and ending the sessions on time.
- Setting the tone and environment for the sessions so that they are warm and comfortable, as well as stimu-lating. You may wish to have a "center piece" (for example, a candle, Bible, and something particularly appropriate for each session).
- Being clear about each week's reading assignment.

- Selecting questions from "Reflections" that are appropriate for your group (or choosing other points of discussion), trusting where the Spirit leads the group.
- Celebrating the different ideas of participants rather than being threatened by them.
- Facilitating group discussion so that 1) everyone has equal opportunities to share, 2) no one feels pressure to share, and 3) no one dominates. (In a group of eight, one-eighth of the discussion time is each person's fair share — including the leader.)
- Closing each session with an attitude of appreciation and care.

Hospitality of the Heart has seven chapters and can be adapted for a study of six, seven, or eight weeks. You may wish to have a special closing, appropriate for your group, during the final session.

- If you plan an eight-week study, use the first session to introduce the book and the format and help participants become acquainted with one another.
- For a seven-week study, the participants should receive the books and read the first chapter in advance.
- For a six-week study, the participants should receive the books and read the first chapter in advance. Choose two chapters to combine, considering the people in the group and your desired objectives.

A WORD FOR PARTICIPANTS

The study of this book offers an opportunity to share together an experience of hospitality of the heart, both giving and receiving hospitality. It includes:

- Praying daily for each other.
- Reading the designated chapter of *Hospitality of the Heart*.
- Trying to practice hospitality in its many facets in various places during the week.

The sessions offer an opportunity to practice hospitality to others in the group by:

- Listening to others with openness and acceptance.
- Valuing individual uniqueness and welcoming fresh perspectives, recognizing that the richness of diversity is a means to growth.
- Facing differences openly and treating one another with respect, applying the RSV translation of Isaiah 1:18: "Come now, let us reason together" rather than that of the NRSV: "Come now, let us argue it out"!
- Honoring requests for confidentiality.

Reflections

Reflections follow for each chapter. If you are reading the book individually, you may want to scan them and ponder the ones meaningful to you. If you are a participant in a study group on hospitality, the reflections can be used as a basis for discussion. See the "Guide for Groups" in the previous section.

GETTING STARTED

- Hospitality ABC: What word do you associate with hospitality that begins with "A"? With "B"? With "C"? See if you can finish the alphabet. You may want to add more words later.
- How do you and your congregation reflect the words you listed?

CHAPTER 1: LOST!

Lesson 1: Hospitality begins with welcoming another as we would welcome the Christ.

- Do you and your congregation tend to welcome others as the Christ? If so, share some examples.
- When you feel "lost," what do you need from others and from your congregation? What do others who feel "lost" need from you?
- How do you and your congregation help answer the prayer: "Lord, help!"?
- Who are your "river rats?" Who are your congregation's "river rats?" How does your congregation (consciously or unconsciously, overtly or subtly) show them that they are not welcome? If you would like to change that, what steps can you take individually and as a congregation to welcome them as the Christ?
- When you are deep in midnight darkness, do you trust that God is there? How does that trust affect your journey through the darkness? How does your congregation help build that trust?

CHAPTER 2:
YOU *CAN'T* DO ANYTHING WRONG HERE

Lesson 2: Hospitality offers the gift of a space and place of grace.

- Is there a person or place that offers you the presence of grace? How can you offer that kind of space, whether you are at home or work or on the spot?
- In what ways is your congregation a space and place of grace? How could it expand its capacity for grace?
- What do you tend to focus on, talk about, and think about when you face toward God? When you face away from God?

- How aware are you of your thoughts? How well do you practice your freedom not to consent to destructive thoughts? How do second thoughts affect your capacity to offer others a space and place of grace?
- How was hospitality in Jesus' culture different from and similar to hospitality today? What new attitudes did Jesus bring to hospitality?
- When you look at a stranger, do you tend to see the face of Jesus? Why or why not? How does xenophobia affect your and your congregation's hospitality?
- Does the media have more influence on your trust level than your own experiences? How does an emphasis on suspicion affect children in a congregation? How can your congregation balance offering a space and place of grace and also providing safety?

CHAPTER 3: WE'VE BEEN TALKING

Lesson 3: Hospitality has the power to bring change both to receiver and giver.

- Has giving or receiving hospitality ever helped change you or your congregation in some way? What are some examples?
- Has giving or receiving hospitality ever helped you or your congregation overcome prejudice or stereotypes? What are some examples? How can the congregation foster these kinds of experiences?
- Which area of hospitality to the self are you most apt to neglect: body, mind, or soul? Would you like to change that? What steps can you take to do so?

- Does your congregation tend toward being more Christ-centered than self-centered? What are some examples?
- How does your congregation foster opportunities to tell stories and share joy, weep and laugh together, hold hands and touch souls?

CHAPTER 4: BEAUTIFUL HANDS

Lesson 4: Hospitality is the measure of beautiful hands.

- What images do you have of beautiful hands? What makes them beautiful to you?
- How can you offer hospitality to God?
- What is missing when you offer hospitality without the heart?
- What is special about offering your hands with your hospitality?
- Consider hospitality in your church:
  - Who is invited to your church? Who's welcome close-up? Those who challenge as well as those who comfort? Down-and-outers? "River rats?"
  - Do overt invitations match subtle wishes? Is there a covert desire among some members to be the big fish even if it means controlling the size of the fishbowl?
  - What kind of invitation is offered? Mass mailing? One-to-one? None?
  - Does seating matter? (Do certain people own certain pews?)
  - How are people welcomed? Is "take-it-or-leave-it" hospitality offered? Are specific individual needs

considered? What efforts are made to help people feel part of the church family?

- What is the underlying tone? Joy and celebration? Criticism and cynicism? Is there a sense of a deep and expansive spiritual life together? Is the space set up to be inviting? Intimidating? Is there a "porch" for lingering and telling stories? Does the tone facilitate transformation?

- Is there a sense that the church belongs to a few members or that all members belong to the church?

- What is the focus? Does the trivial loom large? How is the "table" prepared? What about the center-piece — who is at the *center* (really)?

- How does being deeply Christ-centered affect your and your congregation's hospitality?

- If you want to simplify your life, what "idols" can you discard? What could your congregation discard?

- If you want to stabilize your life, what spiritual seeds would you like to plant?

- How does your congregation celebrate the mystery of God in our scientific, technological, complex world?

- Have you thanked God today for all the beautiful hands that serve you daily, providing you with food (from ground to table), water, clothes, shelter, trans-portation, etc.?

CHAPTER 5: DID YOU GET CANDY?

Lesson 5: Hospitality can transform the ordinary into the extraordinary.

- What blinds you to God's daily gifts? Have you ever glimpsed God's gift but missed the joy? Why?
- Do you and your congregation have too much "candy?" What can you and your congregation do to help balance out the world's "candy?"
- Has greed ever been a destructive force for you or your congregation?
- Do you or your congregation (perhaps unconsciously) have categories of God's children that you think don't deserve "candy?" Would Jesus exclude them?
- How does the media skew the view of certain peoples and problems?
- What is a gift from God that you have received today?

CHAPTER 6: ONE STRAND OF WEB

Lesson 6: God's cosmic hospitality holds us all and connects us together.

- Why do we resist recognizing that all of us dangle together?
- Do you and your congregation refuse to consent to polarization? If so, how? If not, why?
- Is there a special place where you find it easy to connect with God?
- How can you and your congregation show your gratitude for God's cosmic hospitality? How can you become better guests of God?
- What are some ways you and your congregation can "bow" before God and to others?
- What would change in your congregation if you moved "evenly together?"

- Do you and your congregation remember and still forgive? Do you or your congregation need healing in some area? What steps could you take to help bring it about?
- How well do you and your congregation accept and adapt to change? What kinds of changes are the most difficult? What are the benefits of change?

CHAPTER 7: LEAVING HOME

Have you ever felt homeless? What feelings did it stir? What actions?

- Do you have a place that down deep in your heart you call home? What are the feelings you associate with it?
- Can you think of a friend with whom it is easy to feel at home? Why?
- When you feel at home with yourself, what changes? When you feel at home in your congregation, what changes? When you feel at home in the world, what changes?
- Do you agree that when we feel at home with God, home is wherever we are? Why or why not?
- Do you really believe that the table is prepared for you? If so, how can you prepare the table for others?

STARTING ANEW

Take another look at "Hospitality ABC." What words would you add? Would you remove any? How can you enliven them in each starting-anew day, one face of Christ at a time?

Endnotes

CHAPTER 1

[1] John Cassian, "The Conferences of Cassian," *Western Asceticism*,
Owen Chadwick, ed. (Philadelphia: The Westminster Press, 1958),
282.

[2] *The Westminster Dictionary of Christian Spirituality*, Gordon S.
Wakefield, ed. (Philadelphia: The Westminster Press, 1983), 110.

[3] *Western Asceticism*, 145.

[4] *The Sayings of the Desert Fathers: The Alphabetical Collection*,
Benedicta Ward, trans. (Kalamazoo: Cistercian Publications,
1975), 131.

[5] William Ashworth, *The Left Hand of Eden: Meditations on Nature and
Human Nature* (Corvallis, Oregon: Oregon State University Press,
1999), 17.

CHAPTER 2

[1] *Western Asceticism*, 186.

[2] *Seeking a Purer Christian Life: The Desert Mothers and Fathers*, Keith
Beasley-Topliffe, ed. (Nashville: Upper Room Books, 2000), 65.

[3] *The Sayings of the Desert Fathers*, 145

[4] *Ibid.*, 171.

[5] *Seeking a Purer Christian Life*, 44-45.

[6] *The Sayings of the Desert Fathers*, 60.

[7] *Ibid.*, 191.

[8] K. M. George, *The Silent Roots: Orthodox Perspectives on Christian Spirituality* (Geneva: WCC Publications, 1994), 55-56.

[9] Western Asceticism, 184-85.

CHAPTER 3

[1] *The Flowering of the Soul: A Book of Prayers by Women*, Lucinda Vardey, ed. (Vintage Canada, A Division of Random House of Canada Limited), 6.

[2] Thomas Kelly, in a letter to his wife, cited in *The Sanctuary of the Soul: Selected Writings of Thomas Kelly*, Keith Beasley-Topliffe, ed. (Nashville: Upper Room Books, 1997), 14.

[3] *Ibid.*, 24.

[4] *The Rule of St. Benedict: 1980 Abridged Edition* (Collegeville, Minnesota: The Liturgical Press, 1981), 31.

CHAPTER 4

[1] The word *oblate* relates to offering (oblation). Oblates of the Order of St. Benedict are Catholics and non-Catholics who offer their lives to try to live out the Rule of St. Benedict in the secular world.

[2] Simone Weil, "Reflections on the Right Use of School Studies with a View to the Love of God" in *Waiting on God*, Emma Craufurd, trans. (London: HarperCollins, Fount paperback ed., 1959, 1977), 53. Cited in *The Flowering of the Soul*, 6.

[3] *Western Asceticism*, 148.

[4] Esther de Waal, *Seeking God: The Way of St. Benedict* (Collegeville, Minnesota: The Liturgical Press, 1984), 120.

[5] *Ibid.*,120-21.

[6] Ashworth, 123.

CHAPTER 5

[1] Brother David Steindl-Rast, *A Listening Heart: The Spirituality of Sacred Sensuousness* (New York: The Crossroad Publishing Company, 1999), 48.

[2] Joan Chittister, *The Psalms: Meditations for Every Day of the Year* (New York: The Crossroad Publishing Company, 1996), 46.

[3] Ashworth, 77.

[4] W. Paul Jones, *The Province Beyond the River*. Cited in John Killinger, *365 Simple Gifts from God* (Nashville: Dimensions for Living, 1998), 104.

[5] *Western Asceticism*, 186.

[6] Cited in Chittister, 40-41.

CHAPTER 6

[1] From "Ceremonies for Oblates of St. Benedict."

[2] Ashworth, 7.

[3] *Seeking a Purer Christian Life*, 58.

[4] Ashworth, 6.

[5] *Ibid.*, 171

[6] Killinger, 164.

[7] *Seeking a Purer Christian Life*, 46.

[8] Edward M. Hallowell, M.D., *Connect: 12 Vital Ties that Open Your Heart, Lengthen Your Life, and Deepen Your Soul* (New York: Pocket Books,1999), 54-63.

[9] Neil Douglas-Klotz, *Prayers of the Cosmos: Meditations on the Aramaic Words of Jesus* (New York: HarperSanFrancisco, 1994), 65.

[10] Ashworth, 8, 26.

CHAPTER 7

[1] Steindl-Rast, 25.